Reducing Threats at the Source
A European Perspective on Cooperative Threat Reduction

SIPRI Research Report no. 19

Ian Anthony

OXFORD

UNIVERSITY PRESS

Great Clarendon Street, Oxford OX2 6DP
Oxford University Press is a department of the University of Oxford.
It furthers the University's objective of excellence in research, scholarship,
and education by publishing worldwide in

Oxford New York
Auckland Cape Town Dar es Salaam Hong Kong Karachi Kuala Lumpur
Madrid Melbourne Mexico City Nairobi New Delhi Taipei Toronto
Shanghai
With offices in
Argentina Austria Brazil Chile Czech Republic France Greece
Guatemala Hungary Italy Japan South Korea Poland Portugal
Singapore Switzerland Thailand Turkey Ukraine Vietnam

Oxford is a registered trade mark of Oxford University Press
in the UK and certain other countries

Published in the United States
by Oxford University Press Inc., New York

© SIPRI 2004

First published 2004

British Library Cataloguing in Publication Data
Data available

Library of Congress Cataloging in Publication Data
Data available

ISBN 0-19-927177-1
ISBN 0-19-927178-X (pbk)

6 4 2 3 5 7

Typeset and originated by Stockholm International Peace Research Institute
Printed in Great Britain on acid-free paper by
Biddles Ltd., King's Lynn, Norfolk

90 0613484 9

Reducing Threats at the Source

A European Perspective on Cooperative Threat Reduction

Contents

Preface

The United States and Russia began a Cooperative Threat Reduction (CTR) programme in 1991 to try to control the colossal process of dismantling and making safe former-Soviet capacities for non-conventional warfare after the end of the cold war. After a decade, this endeavour was starting to run out of steam as some problems were relegated to history and stubborn blockages frustrated the effort to tackle others. In common with many other fields of security, 11 September 2001 changed all that. The newly dominant concern about mass-impact terrorism, linked with the nightmare of terrorist access to weapons of mass destruction, put the 'threat' back into cooperative threat reduction overnight. All the G8 countries pledged themselves in June 2002 to the Global Partnership Against the Spread of Weapons and Materials of Mass Destruction, an initiative designed to drive forward the work of eliminating, controlling or converting the most hazardous capacities on a grand scale. Related policy themes and activities in other important institutional frameworks such as the European Union, the North Atlantic Treaty Organization and the International Atomic Energy Agency were given new priority and funding.

This renaissance in CTR-like work has made it one of the most significant and interesting lines of international activity contributing both to the general aims of disarmament and arms control and to the consolidation of cooperation and trust between old enemies. It has also raised new questions to add to old ones that were not resolved in the previous decade. What are the bounds of CTR and how does it relate to control and destruction efforts driven by other, for instance, environmental concerns? How strong in reality is the linkage with terrorism and what could be the pitfalls of elevating it to the programme's *raison d'être*? Are current activities sufficiently and appropriately coordinated among nations and institutions and at the domestic level by the recipient countries—notably, Russia? How can the effectiveness of project selection and design, choice of agents and resource application be measured? Can we be sure, in short, that the very large sums pledged for the new Global Partnership will be sensibly and transparently used?

SIPRI's Research Coordinator, Ian Anthony, approaches this subject from a background combining research experience, participation in key policy-forming projects and hands-on experience of the Russian environment. His analysis brings out the problems, deficiencies and elements of confusion inherent in current CTR endeavours but makes a strong case for broadening, strengthening and deepening these efforts rather than giving up on a concept, so fertile for addressing current security needs.

This Research Report deserves careful reading by all who are engaged in CTR and Global Partnership activities, whether from the public or the private sector. Thanks are due for its timely production to Ian himself and to SIPRI editor Andy Mash.

Alyson J. K. Bailes
Director, SIPRI
March 2004

Acronyms

AMEC	Arctic Military Environmental Cooperation
BEAC	Barents Euro–Arctic Council
BTWC	Biological and Toxin Weapons Convention
BW	Biological weapon
CBSS	Council of Baltic Sea States
CBW	Chemical and biological weapons
CFSP	Common Foreign and Security Policy
CIS	Commonwealth of Independent States
CPPNM	Convention on Physical Protection of Nuclear Material
CTR	Cooperative threat reduction
CW	Chemical weapon
CWC	Chemical Weapons Convention
DOE	Department of Energy (US)
EAEC	European Atomic Energy Community (Euratom)
ETRI	Expanded Threat Reduction Initiative
EU	European Union
FSU	Former Soviet Union
GIS	Group of Interested States
G7	Group of Seven
G8	Group of Eight
HEU	Highly enriched uranium
IAEA	International Atomic Energy Agency
ISTC	International Science and Technology Center
MANPADS	Man-portable air defence weapons
MINATOM	Ministry of Atomic Energy (Russia)
MNEPR	Multilateral Nuclear Environmental Programme in the Russian Federation
NAMSA	NATO Maintenance and Supply Agency
NATO	North Atlantic Treaty Organization
NBC	Nuclear, biological and chemical (weapons)
NDCI	Non-Proliferation and Disarmament Cooperation Initiative
NDEP	Northern Dimension Environmental Partnership
NGO	Non-governmental organization
NPT	Non-Proliferation Treaty
NSDC	National Security and Defence Council

PFP	Partnership for Peace
PMSC	Political-Military Steering Committee (on Partnership for Peace)
SALW	Small arms and light weapons
SGP	Senior Politico-Military Group on Proliferation (NATO)
SORT	Strategic Offensive Reductions Treaty
START	Strategic Arms Reduction Treaty
TACIS	Technical Assistance for the Commonwealth of Independent States
UN	United Nations
UNDP	UN Development Programme
USSR	Union of Soviet Socialist Republics, Soviet Union
WMD	Weapon of mass destruction

1. Introduction

I. Background

At their summit meeting in Kananaskis, Canada, in June 2002 the Heads of State and Government of the Group of Eight (G8) industrialized countries announced a Global Partnership Against the Spread of Weapons and Materials of Mass Destruction (Global Partnership) to provide assistance to states (in the first instance the Russian Federation) that lack the means to implement shared disarmament, nonproliferation and counter-terrorism objectives.[1] This partnership was broadened in June and July 2003 when six countries that are not members of the G8 (Finland, the Netherlands, Norway, Poland, Sweden and Switzerland) joined it.[2]

The timing of the G8 initiative, which builds on an agreement reached by Germany and the United States in talks between US President George W. Bush and German Chancellor Gerhard Schröder, was heavily influenced by the terrorist attacks on the USA on 11 September 2001.[3] In the statement accompanying their decision to establish the Global Partnership the G8 leaders underlined that, because the attacks on the USA had demonstrated that terrorists were prepared to use any means to inflict mass casualties on innocent people, it was essential 'to prevent terrorists, or those that harbour them, from acquiring or developing nuclear, chemical, radiological and biological weapons, missiles and related materials, equipment and technology.[4]

The Kananaskis meeting was the first G8 Summit after the terrorist attacks on the USA. A strong statement on the need to combat terror-

---

[1] The G8 is an informal group in which Canada, France, Germany, Italy, Japan, Russia, the UK and the USA as well as the European Union (EU) participate. The EU is represented by the President of the European Commission and by the leader of the country that holds the presidency of the Council of the European Union at the time of the G8 summit meeting.

[2] US Mission to the European Union, 'Netherlands Joins Global Partnership Against the Spread of WMD', Brussels, Belgium, 11 July 2003, URL <http://www.useu.be/Categories/Defense/June1103NetherlandsWMD.html>.

[3] German Ministry of Foreign Affairs, 'Der deutsche Beitrag zur G8-Globalen Partnerschaft gegen die Verbreitung von Massenvernichtungswaffen und materialien' [The German contribution to the G8 Global Partnership Against the Spread of Weapons and Materials of Mass Destruction], 7 July 2003, URL <http://www.diplo.de/www/de/aussenpolitik/friedens politik/abr_und_r/aktuell_massenvernichtungswaffen_html>.

[4] Statement by G8 leaders, 'The Global Partnership Against the Spread of Weapons and Materials of Mass Destruction', Kananaskis, Canada, 27 June 2002, URL <http://www.g8.gc.ca/2002Kananaskis/kananaskis/globpart-en.asp>.

ism was to be expected from G8 leaders. The G8 partners agreed to develop specific measures to enhance counter-terrorism cooperation. The Global Partnership is partly intended to meet this commitment in that either enhanced physical security for, or the physical elimination of, nuclear, biological and chemical (NBC) weapons, radiological weapons, and missile delivery systems for these weapons, as well as NBC and missile-related materials, equipment and technology, would deny such items to terrorists. The decisions taken at Kananaskis and afterwards are not just political statements. They are expected to generate a large, diverse and costly programme of work to be implemented in Russia and in other countries over the course of at least the next decade.

The political decision by the G8 leaders is expected to translate into a significant commitment of national resources from each participant in the Global Partnership. In public statements the G8 leaders made a political commitment to raise up to $20 billion over 10 years. The types of measures that may be supported by the Global Partnership are those usually associated with Cooperative Threat Reduction (CTR). Originally, CTR was the name of a specific programme managed by the US Department of Defense.[5] The acronym has now come to be used both in Russia and elsewhere to cover a wide range of practical measures intended 'to reduce the dangers posed by the old Soviet Union's massive cold war arsenals' where these measures involve international assistance.[6]

The timing, scale and scope of the Global Partnership commitment were all surprising in certain respects. Political support for CTR had begun to wane in the USA from the late 1990s onwards because the problems that it was intended to address appeared less acute in the eyes of many observers. Moreover, doubts were increasingly raised about the effectiveness of the external efforts that were being undertaken in Russia—the primary focus of CTR programmes.

---

[5] The US Cooperative Threat Reduction (CTR) programme is managed by the US Department of Defense (DOD) within the framework of the 1991 Soviet Nuclear Threat Reduction Act (also known as the Nunn–Lugar Act after the senators who co-sponsored the original authorizing legislation). The programme subsequently evolved to encompass a wide range of non-proliferation and demilitarization activities under the auspices of the Department of Energy, the Department of State and the DOD.

[6] Luongo, K. and Hoehn, W. E., 'Reform and expansion of cooperative threat reduction', *Arms Control Today*, vol. 33, no. 5 (June 2003), p. 11.

From the mid-1990s, after a number of incidents suggested a growing willingness by Chechen groups to use radiological materials to commit terrorist acts,[7] Russia itself began to take measures to secure the materials and facilities considered to be at greatest risk. At the same time, many external cooperation projects were experiencing implementation difficulties because of obstruction from senior officials in Russia who believed that CTR was neither welcome nor in Russia's true interests, rather than because of any genuine technical problems.[8] While the impact of some projects was difficult to measure, there was also a feeling that monitoring effectiveness was more difficult than necessary because of the lack of information provided by Russian authorities.[9]

The projects carried out to facilitate the destruction of nuclear and chemical weapons in Russia have their origins in a threat scenario based on a risk of large-scale armed conflict between the USA and Russia. While CTR began as an emergency programme in response to the rapid collapse of the Union of Soviet Socialist Republics (USSR), subsequent projects have largely been undertaken to help implement commitments contained in arms control agreements—the first bilateral Russian–US strategic arms reduction treaty, the 1991 START I Treaty,[10] and the 1993 Chemical Weapons Convention (CWC),

---

[7] The Radon enterprise in Chechnya maintained a site at which medium- and low-level radioactive waste was buried during the Soviet period. In 1995 a Chechen separatist group buried a device containing 32 kg of Caesium-137, a radioactive metal, in Ismailovsky Park, Moscow. The device was recovered without any radiation leakage. Federal troops took responsibility for safeguarding the security of waste stored at Radon. 'Russian general: Chechen nuclear waste plant under control', ITAR-TASS (Moscow), 1 Mar. 2000, in Foreign Broadcast Information Service, *Daily Report–Central Eurasia (FBIS-SOV)*, FBIS-SOV-2000-0301, 2 Mar. 2000.

[8] This issue is discussed in detail in chapter 3.

[9] CTR already had its critics by 1996. See, e.g., Kelly, R., 'The Nunn–Lugar Act: a wasteful and dangerous illusion', *Cato Foreign Policy Briefing*, no. 39 (18 Mar. 1996). Many of the same criticisms were made subsequently by, e.g., the US General Accounting Office (GAO) and the Congressional Research Service (CRS), 'Weapons of mass destruction: US efforts to reduce threats from the former Soviet Union', Testimony of Harold J. Johnson, GAO Associate Director, International Relations and Trade Issues, National Security and International Affairs Division, to the Subcommittee on Emerging Threats and Capabilities, Committee on Armed Services, US Senate, 6 Mar. 2000; and Woolf, A. F., *Nunn–Lugar Cooperative Threat Reduction Programs: Issues for Congress*, Report for Congress, (CRS: Washington, DC, 23 Mar. 2001).

[10] The 1991 US–Russian/Soviet Treaty on the Reduction and Limitation of Strategic Offensive Arms (START I Treaty), which entered into force on 5 Dec. 1994. The treaty obliges the parties to make phased reductions in their offensive strategic nuclear forces over a 7-year period. It sets numerical limits on deployed strategic nuclear delivery vehicles, intercontinental ballistic missiles, submarine-launched ballistic missiles and heavy bombers—and

respectively.[11] By 2000 the START I Treaty had been almost fully implemented and the need for such implementation assistance in Russia and Ukraine was declining.

In these circumstances there was a growing view that CTR had achieved what could reasonably have been expected from it. In the face of a loss of focus about future programme objectives, and with implementation bottlenecks being highlighted, it appeared logical that CTR would be phased out and the resources diverted to other uses.

Against this background, it becomes clear that the decision to revitalize the discussion of CTR was a direct result of the intense shock created by the attacks of 11 September 2001, following which there was an immediate and urgent search for measures to help achieve non-proliferation and counter-terrorism objectives. However, if it is viewed only in this context, strengthening CTR in the manner suggested by the Global Partnership risks coming to be seen as a 'knee-jerk' reaction that, while understandable in its context, is in reality diverting resources away from more promising approaches to non-proliferation and counter-terrorism.

On closer inspection, there have been relatively few CTR projects that relate directly to the threat scenarios of greatest concern, if seen through the prism of non-proliferation or counter-terrorism.

The strategic nuclear systems, the main focus for CTR projects, would have been the least likely to be transferred to any other country and would have been very badly suited to the needs of terrorist groups—even in the highly remote contingency that they had been able to gain access to and control of such systems after their consolidation in Russia. Similarly, assistance to destroy chemical weapons (CW) does relatively little to contribute to objectives related to non-proliferation and counter-terrorism. The transfer of sufficient chemical munitions from Russia to be of military significance to another

the nuclear warheads they carry. In the Protocol to Facilitate the Implementation of the START Treaty (1992 Lisbon Protocol), which entered into force on 5 Dec. 1994, Belarus, Kazakhstan and, in particular, Ukraine also assumed the obligations of the former Soviet Union under the treaty. They pledged to eliminate all the former Soviet strategic nuclear weapons on their territories within the 7-year reduction period and to join the 1968 Non-Proliferation Treaty as non-nuclear weapon states in the shortest possible time.

[11] The 1993 Convention on the Prohibition of the Development, Production, Stockpiling and Use of Chemical Weapons and on their Destruction (Chemical Weapons Convention, CWC), which entered into force on 29 Apr. 1997. Each party undertakes to destroy its chemical weapons and production facilities within 10 years of the entry into force of the convention.

state is extremely unlikely to be possible without the connivance of the Russian authorities, which would be a clear and detectable breach of the CWC. While certainly serious, the acquisition of one or a small number of chemical munitions by a non-state group would be a relatively low-level threat in comparison with other actions that could be taken by terrorist groups with relatively greater ease.

None of the projects scheduled to commence their implementation phase in the short term emphasizes international cooperation to track, quantify, secure and eliminate nuclear weapons that are not subject to an arms reduction agreement, or the weapon-grade material from those weapons. None of the projects developed or implemented with Russia directly addresses the issue of biological weapons (BW), and even the number of projects that could have an indirect impact on BW-related concerns has been relatively low.

These observations are not intended to suggest that there is no need for CTR efforts. On the contrary, such efforts can make a very important contribution to building security. However, it will be necessary to translate political statements into money and projects and then to sustain that commitment over a long period in order to assist Russia and other countries to address the problems they face. This sustained commitment will only be forthcoming if identified project requirements match the main anticipated security priorities. It is arguable that states—in particular European states—will be more likely to develop a sustainable CTR programme if these political priorities take into account a wider set of issues and a larger group of countries than those that might be identified with direct reference to the immediate needs of the existing CTR programme.

Measures such as those envisaged in the Global Partnership are one—but only one—example of a willingness by states to render practical assistance to one another to help manage security problems. A significant number of such practical assistance projects are being conducted in different places around the world, although not necessarily focused on the same weapons or items that have been the mainstay of CTR.

Taken collectively, these practical assistance projects have not been conducted as part of an overall concept or agreed framework and there is therefore no shared understanding of what is meant by the term CTR. Moreover, and not unrelated to the lack of conceptual clarity, there is no comprehensive inventory of the problems that need to be addressed or of projects that it would be necessary to undertake to be confident that the overall effort is making a substantial contribution to non-proliferation and counter-terrorism.

II. The nature of cooperative threat reduction measures

A broad definition of CTR would be 'practical measures to enhance security jointly implemented and with consent on the territory of one state by a coalition of parties that may include states, international organizations, local and regional government, non-governmental organizations (NGOs) and the private sector'. This functional definition does not assume that practical assistance is limited to any particular threat, in keeping with the fact that assistance has been and is being provided not only in the name of non-proliferation and counter-terrorism but also to achieve other military and non-military security objectives. This definition also disconnects the issue from any particular location and from the issue of NBC weapons.

Cooperative threat reduction cannot be said to be exclusively a part of traditional military security since it also contains aspects, such as environmental protection and nuclear safety, that have no traditional military dimension. Some of the projects that have been carried out in the military domain have been undertaken primarily to support environmental protection objectives while some projects in the civilian nuclear power sector have been undertaken to alleviate military security concerns.

In broad terms, military CTR activities have been of three types: facilitating the dismantlement and destruction of weapons, the establishment of a chain of custody over weapons or other items, and demilitarization and conversion projects.

Projects have been carried out that are intended to account for, consolidate and secure weapons, materials, technology and know-how (including individual scientists and engineers) related to nuclear and chemical weapons as well as missile delivery systems intended to deliver nuclear weapons. In addition to the transport, storage and dismantlement of nuclear warheads and delivery vehicles, nuclear-related CTR projects have been developed to help account for and safely store fissile material that could be used to make nuclear weapons and to dispose of one such material (highly enriched uranium, HEU) by finding alternative uses for it. The destruction of CW has also been an important priority.

While these projects are all prompted by military security concerns, the term CTR has also been applied to activities to safeguard and control items and materials that are not weapons in the traditional sense—such as nuclear waste and other radioactive materials. In addition, there have been projects related to nuclear waste management and to enhancing the physical security of radioactive source material in storage and during transport. For example, the removal of fuel assemblies from the reactors that propel nuclear submarines has been an important priority within CTR. However, these submarines, which have been taken out of service by the Russian Navy and cannot realistically be restored to working condition, represent an environmental hazard rather than a military threat. Moreover, because some of the fuel assemblies contain uranium that has been enriched to over 30 per cent (and in some cases to over 90 per cent), their removal could create not only an even greater environmental risk but also a potential proliferation risk, if they were not securely stored.[12]

Demilitarization projects have included efforts to convert military facilities to civilian use, including the promotion of international joint ventures and related access to the international market for civil products from these facilities. Demilitarization projects have also sought to provide alternative employment for scientists previously employed in NBC programmes. These efforts have been characterized as CTR (even though these projects must be civilian in orientation if they are to achieve their intended results) because of the contribution they make to achieving NBC non-proliferation. Other demilitarization efforts, such as assisting with the demobilization of strategic rocket forces personnel in Ukraine by providing them with housing, do not directly contribute to non-proliferation objectives and have more of a humanitarian or 'social security' character. However, these projects have proved to be a valuable indirect element of the overall effort to reduce proliferation risks since without them it might not have been possible to gain acceptance for the overall programme.

Cooperative threat reduction is not an activity that has been the preserve of any single institution or organization. Projects have been dis-

---

[12] Technical issues surrounding naval nuclear propulsion systems are described in Krupnick, C., *Decommissioned Russian Nuclear Submarines and International Cooperation* (McFarland and Company: Jefferson, N.C., 2001).

cussed and developed *inter alia* in international organizations and more informal settings. The discussions have included states, international organizations as well as local government, the private sector of industry and NGOs. Nor is CTR an activity that is confined to one country. Although most of the projects usually considered to come under this label have been carried out in Russia there have also been projects in other countries, most notably Ukraine, but also Belarus, Kazakhstan and Uzbekistan.

The functional definition offered above assumes that the overarching objectives of CTR projects are to be established in other processes. Projects can help to implement a policy agenda but, even if undertaken collectively, they do not establish one. In practice, in the past CTR has reached back into other processes for elements that are needed for successful project implementation. The most extensive and successful CTR projects have been coupled to the implementation of arms control and disarmament agreements, notably the START I Treaty and the CWC.

This relationship, in which CTR measures are implementing an agenda established elsewhere, is also discernible in the field of environmental protection, where discussions in northern Europe have led to the progressive development of agreed objectives that have subsequently been absorbed into the Northern Dimension for the Policies of the Union—part of the European Union (EU) Common Foreign and Security Policy (CFSP).[13] These objectives and, more recently, decisions about a legal framework for cooperation are, in turn, expected to assist the design and development of successful projects. In another example, in the field of nuclear safety and accounting for and securing radiological materials, the International Atomic Energy Agency (IAEA), a specialized agency of the United Nations, has played a key role in the development of agreed standards that particular projects can use as a point of reference.[14]

---

[13] The Northern Dimension was established at the European Council meeting in Dec. 1998 based on the European Commission, Communication on a Northern Dimension for the Policies of the Union, COM/98/0589 Final, Brussels, 25 Nov. 1998, available at URL <http://europa.eu.int/comm/external_relations/north_dim/doc/com1998_0589en.pdf>.

[14] The IAEA was established as an autonomous organization under the UN in 1957. The Statute of the IAEA is available at <http://www.iaea.org/About/statute_text.html>.

Because the design of specific CTR projects will be shaped by the objectives established in these different processes, it is important that those objectives are not contradictory. For example, demilitarization projects should not undermine environmental protection and, equally, environmental protection should not increase the risk of weapon proliferation or lead to the stockpiling of dangerous materials in secure facilities.

III. Arms control and cooperative threat reduction

The USA has been carrying out CTR assistance programmes in Russia and in other countries of the former Soviet Union (FSU) since 1991. The initial objective was to address the most immediate military security threats to the USA created by the legacy of the massive militarization that took place in the USSR during the cold war.

In November 1991, when the US CTR programme was initiated, there were significant risks associated with the collapse of the communist bloc. Following the dissolution of the Warsaw Treaty Organization and the collapse of the USSR large numbers of personnel, weapons and items of military equipment were taken out of service and/or moved to new locations. Under the prevailing conditions an emergency programme was considered essential to reduce, and if possible eliminate, the risk that physical control would be lost over the enormous arsenal of weapons and associated infrastructure accumulated by the USSR during the cold-war period. Attention was focused on what were considered to be the most dangerous weapons from a US perspective.

In the prevailing conditions, European countries also saw great risks to their own security should control over nuclear weapons be lost or new nuclear weapon powers emerge in Europe. France and the United Kingdom (both nuclear weapon states) as well as Germany contributed directly to the consolidation of Soviet nuclear weapons in Russia through the provision of specialist equipment between 1992 and 1994 in order to ensure that the process was accomplished as quickly and efficiently as possible.[15]

While CTR was initially seen as a temporary programme established to focus on ensuring that nuclear weapons were secure and accounted for while being transported, disassembled and stored, the

[15] See note 10. This consolidation process is discussed further below.

programme was extended after 1991 to support projects that assisted with the implementation of formal arms control agreements. Initially, this expansion took place in the nuclear domain but, after Russia signed the CWC in 1993, assisting it to implement its CW disarmament obligations became an important focus for CTR efforts. Russia signed the CWC in the expectation that there would be significant external assistance to help it comply with agreed destruction deadlines.[16]

The objective of arms control is to ensure self-restraint with regard to national military capabilities and to decisions that could support the development of military capabilities by other states. These restraint measures include the reduction or elimination of capabilities created in the past but for which no useful purpose is envisaged. Arms control places the full legal responsibility for implementing any agreed measures on the state party to any agreement. However, past experience has shown that states parties which fully intend to meet their obligations can face practical barriers to doing so. In this regard CTR can help to achieve arms control objectives by overcoming barriers to arms control treaty implementation.

Ever since the early 1990s powerful interest groups in Russia, including the armed forces, have been reluctant to give arms control implementation a high priority in relation to other programmes when allocating the limited national resources available. In making their decisions about resource allocation, the military have tried to support the modernization and renewal of the force structure rather than its dismantlement. Threat reduction projects have been used as an important incentive to try to persuade the Russian and Ukrainian military and other influential bodies—including the respective parliaments—of the importance of treaty implementation.

In practical terms, the existence of arms control agreements created an environment in which project implementation became easier. The arms control treaties include detailed understandings on the information that should be collected and exchanged on specific items of equipment. The arrangements for verification include provisions for inspections and establish a right of access for inspectors. All these

---

[16] Kalinina, N., 'Effectiveness of Chemical Weapons Convention depends on Russia's actions, *Yarderny Kontrol*, vol. 9, no. 1 (spring 2003), pp. 94–95, available (in Russian) at URL <http://www.pircenter.org/data/publications/yk1-2003.pdf>.

elements were codified in agreements signed by the head of state and ratified by the national parliament. This framework meant that issues related to the provision of information and the granting of physical access, which if not managed successfully could delay or obstruct the implementation of CTR projects, were resolved in the most clear and definitive manner.

Arms control and CTR have features that make them different but compatible and complementary activities. The relationship between the two types of activity is not straightforward. This complicated relationship is mirrored in actual experience.

While arms control is highly state-centric, CTR is likely to be implemented by a mix of state and non-state actors.

Unlike arms control treaties, which usually create symmetrical obligations among the states that are party to them, CTR is highly asymmetrical. The existence of arms control agreements went at least some way to reducing the concern that CTR was a discriminatory activity that disadvantaged the country in which projects were based. Nevertheless, CTR programmes do involve specific and differentiated activities tailored to the conditions prevailing in each location where projects are carried out. While arms control requires the exchange of information, it is a characteristic of CTR programmes that information has flowed out from the country in which projects are being implemented without the requirement for reciprocity.

The issue of asymmetry has played a significant role in the discussion of CTR in Russia, where the development of greater reciprocal access to information and activities in the USA has sometimes been advocated as a confidence-building measure.[17]

The legislation that set up the original US CTR programme established the following objectives:[18] (a) to destroy nuclear, chemical, and other weapons of mass destruction (WMD); (b) to transport, store,

---

[17] One recent study has observed that 'the problem is that the CTR program operates as a US assistance program in Russia, so the Russians do not have the same opportunities to develop relationships at US elimination facilities. In effect, they lack the natural transparency that accrues from these relationships. In an ideal world, Russian companies would have an equal right to compete on contracts to eliminate US weapons systems. In practice, however, this outcome is highly unlikely, given the competitiveness of US defense contracting. Some small subcontracts might be awarded, e.g., to dispose of scrap metal. Nevertheless, Russian experts have argued that even a small symbolic project of this type would do much to bolster confidence in Moscow'. Dvorkin, V. *et al.*, Institute for Applied International Research (IAIR), 'From mutual deterrence to a Russian–American partnership: issues demanding resolution', *IAIR Policy Papers*, vol. 2, no. 3 (IAIR: Moscow, Mar. 2003), p. 8.

[18] See note 5.

disable and safeguard weapons in connection with their destruction; (c) to establish verifiable safeguards against proliferation of such weapons; (d) to prevent diversion of weapon-related expertise; (e) to facilitate demilitarization of defence industries and conversion of military capabilities and technologies; and (f) to expand defence and military contacts between the USA and the states that emerged on the territory of the FSU. The success in achieving these objectives has been mixed.

After the 1991 START I Treaty entered into force in December 1994, Russia was required to limit its strategic nuclear forces to no more than 6000 accountable warheads on no more than 1600 strategic delivery vehicles. Russia made it clear to the USA from the outset that assistance with warhead dismantlement was neither wanted nor needed and US–Russian projects have not directly dismantled any nuclear warheads. However, the CTR programme has tried to help Russia to implement its nuclear arms control commitments by developing systems to account for warheads, consolidating warheads in known locations, and making certain that they are technically safe and physically secure during transportation and storage. Projects have also made a more direct contribution to dismantling and destroying the systems—bombers, missiles, land-based missile silos and submarine launch-platforms—in Russia and Ukraine that were to have been used to deliver strategic nuclear weapons.

While CTR has played an indirect role in helping Russia to reduce its overall nuclear weapon arsenal, it is not possible to make a precise calculation of the impact because the size and shape of this arsenal is not known outside Russia. Many Russian nuclear weapons are not subject to arms control agreements. An authoritative statement on the aggregate number of Russian nuclear warheads is not therefore available.

Of the 30 000 nuclear warheads estimated to have been in the Russian arsenal in 1992, CTR activities have probably facilitated the elimination of around 6000 by 2003.[19] However, this can only be a tentative statement since the counting rules applied in the START I

---

[19] For a discussion of the likely size of the Russian nuclear arsenal in 2003, see Kristensen, H. M. and Kile, S. N., 'World nuclear forces', *SIPRI Yearbook 2003: Armaments, Disarmament and International Security* (Oxford University Press: Oxford, 2003), pp. 615–17.

Treaty were derived from the maximum capacities of delivery systems rather than from an accurate count of total warheads. Moreover, in addition to implementing the START I Treaty, Russia is believed to have eliminated an undisclosed number of weapons unilaterally following political undertakings made by the President of the USSR, Mikhail Gorbachev, in October 1991 and the President of the Russian Federation, Boris Yeltsin, in January 1992.[20]

The CTR measures intended to help establish a chain of custody over nuclear weapons, fissile materials and other nuclear materials have played an important role in supporting other arms control agreements. The implementation of the START I Treaty included the consolidation of over 1200 nuclear warheads that had been stored in Belarus, Kazakhstan and Ukraine and the transportation of these warheads to storage facilities in Russia. CTR also facilitated the elimination of strategic delivery systems for these weapons in Ukraine. It is impossible to know whether it would have been possible to persuade these three countries to sign the 1968 Non-Proliferation Treaty (NPT)[21] as non-nuclear weapon states, which they did in May 1992, in the absence of incentives, including the assistance provided through CTR.

In the absence of an arms control framework, or where the good faith intention to implement existing arms control agreements is lacking or contested, CTR does not bring about arms reductions. This has been illustrated in the areas of chemical and biological weapons (CBW). In June 1990 the USA and the USSR agreed that the destruction of their respective CW stockpiles would begin at the end of 1992 and, as noted above, facilitating the implementation of this agreement was an objective of the original US CTR programme. However, this informal bilateral agreement was not implemented prior to the entry into force of the CWC in 1997. While Russia did develop a draft chemical demilitarization programme, it was never adopted. Consequently, no CW-related CTR activities could be defined prior to Russia's signature of the CWC, at which point Russia took on a legal

---

[20] 'The 1991–92 US, Soviet and Russian unilateral nuclear reduction initiatives', *SIPRI Yearbook 1992: World Armaments and Disarmament* (Oxford University Press: Oxford, 1992), pp. 85–92. These initiatives are discussed in Fieldhouse, R., 'Nuclear weapon developments and unilateral reduction initiatives', *SIPRI Yearbook 1992*, pp. 71–73. It is estimated that between 5000 and 15 000 non-strategic warheads have been destroyed by Russia.

[21] The 1968 Treaty on the Non-proliferation of Nuclear Weapons, which entered into force on 5 Mar. 1970.

obligation to destroy its stockpiles and argued that the bilateral agreement was no longer meaningful.

In spite of efforts to address at least some concerns about Russian BW-related activities through CTR, a number of governments— including the UK and the USA—have never been fully satisfied that suspect activities are not taking place in Russia. While the wider failure to verify Russian compliance with the 1972 Biological and Toxin Weapons Convention (BTWC)[22] has not been remedied, CTR projects have probably proved useful in indirect ways.

Cooperative threat reduction has been linked to efforts to prevent the proliferation of BW by preventing a scientific 'brain drain' to countries of concern as well as supporting training programmes designed to help convert military facilities to civilian use and assist with implementing export controls.

Promoting alternative uses for economic assets in the defence sector helps to facilitate arms control indirectly by reducing pressure to maintain a military establishment larger than that required to safeguard national security. Moreover, activities to provide scientists previously working in the defence industry with alternative employment may have helped to prevent the diversion of weapon-related expertise. However, neither of these indirect benefits is possible to validate or quantify.

Projects have helped to achieve demilitarization and BTWC compliance more directly in both Kazakhstan and Uzbekistan, where the USSR had located parts of its extensive BW complex.

Future linkages between arms control and cooperative threat reduction

This brief overview suggests that there have certainly been synergies between arms control and CTR in the past. Future opportunities for such beneficial interactions between the two processes are probably limited, however, because recent arms control treaties lack those elements that were beneficial to CTR efforts.

---

[22] The 1972 Convention on the Prohibition of the Development, Production and Stockpiling of Bacteriological (Biological) and Toxin Weapons and on their Destruction (Biological and Toxin Weapons Convention, BTWC), which entered into force on 26 Mar. 1975.

The Russian–US Strategic Offensive Reductions Treaty (SORT)[23] requires the two sides to reduce their nuclear forces to levels within an agreed range of 1700–2200 warheads by 2012. Under the treaty, which refers to warhead numbers, synergies with CTR measures related to fissile material might be expected. The dismantlement of warheads will produce quantities of fissile material that will need to be put into safe and secure storage. This should, ideally, be followed by disposal. However, the SORT Treaty does not include agreements on information exchange and inspection that could facilitate CTR projects.[24] Therefore, the Russian military establishment is not required to provide either information about or access to facilities, which would be necessary for verification in the normal sense. Historical experience suggests that, in the absence of a legal obligation, such access and information will not be provided.[25]

During the negotiations that led to the SORT Treaty the Russian Government indicated that it intended to implement the treaty by using the same counting concepts developed for START and then to eliminate or convert missile and heavy bomber delivery systems. Given the continued economic constraints within which the Russian armed forces will have to operate, CTR programmes might be useful to facilitate the elimination of delivery systems considered surplus by the Russian armed forces.

The negotiation of a treaty banning the future production of fissile material for weapon purposes—a prerequisite for both nuclear disarmament and effective nuclear non-proliferation—is currently an important arms control objective.[26] Although negotiations have not yet begun, an effective fissile material control and accountancy process that would allow a confident statement of how much fissile material exists for nuclear weapon use would be an essential element of a fissile material treaty. Such a system will be required to deter-

[23] The 2002 Strategic Offensive Reductions Treaty, which entered into force on 1 June 2003.

[24] The USA initially resisted Russia's calls for reductions to be codified in a legally binding agreement, but later acquiesced. Russia, in return, agreed to terms that maximized the flexibility of the parties in implementing the arms cuts. Kile, S. N., 'Nuclear arms control, non-proliferation and ballistic missile defence', *SIPRI Yearbook 2003* (note 19), pp. 600–03.

[25] The serious obstacles that currently exist to enhancing transparency are analysed in Zarimpas, N. (ed.), SIPRI, *Transparency in Nuclear Warheads and Materials: The Political and Technical Dimensions* (Oxford University Press: Oxford, 2003).

[26] The controversy surrounding the negotiation of a possible Fissile Material Cut-off Treaty is discussed in Zarimpas (note 25).

mine that the identified stockpile is not being added to through new production. The development of effective fissile material protection, control and accounting procedures has been examined in US–Russian CTR projects.

IV. Environmental protection and cooperative threat reduction

During the cold war the discussion of military threats—the danger that the armed forces of adversarial states would fight one another with enormously destructive consequences—dominated thinking about security in Europe. After the end of the cold war the effort to address military threats was supplemented by efforts to tackle a range of identified common problems with the potential to cause damage. Addressing non-military aspects of security became both necessary and inevitable for European countries as they began to reopen the full range of contacts among themselves that had been impossible during the cold war. Within the very broad range of contacts initiated, a few have relevance for the discussion of CTR.

The cooperation that was initiated in northern Europe during this period was consciously conceived as a part of a 'soft security policy' towards Russia. European countries played a central role in defining this soft security agenda—a logical development given their greater vulnerability to threats emanating from the FSU. This agenda has included concerns about a range of threats to the environment.

While Russian military-related nuclear activities are among the list of problems identified by Russia's neighbours, environmental aspects of the soft security agenda have also included mitigating the anticipated effects of climate change and the negative impact of industrial pollution with a special emphasis on chemicals, persistent organic pollutants, toxic waste, heavy metals and urban waste—a significantly wider range of issues than those usually grouped under the heading of CTR. Russian heavy industry, in particular in the heavy metals and chemical sectors, raises environmental concerns on a level similar to those in the nuclear sector. Therefore, from an environmental protection perspective, there has been no compelling reason to concentrate exclusively on nuclear matters and, from a practical standpoint, it has been easier to make progress in other areas where barriers to project implementation are lower.

Unlike the case of arms control, where a set of agreements and an institutional structure for implementing those agreements was developed during the cold war, the discussion of a regional system for environmental protection had to be developed from scratch. Moreover, the international legal framework for environmental protection was much less well developed than the arms control framework at the time CTR became politically feasible.

Nevertheless, the need to enhance nuclear safety has been an important element of this overall approach. Nuclear safety means ensuring that there is no undue risk to the health and safety of the general public and site personnel from the operation of nuclear installations, including nuclear power plants, research reactors, parts of the nuclear fuel cycle and related infrastructure. However, the drafting of the Convention on Nuclear Safety,[27] which was adopted in June 1994, did not begin until 1992.

Following the Chernobyl accident in 1986, European countries sought to raise the level of safety at nuclear installations in Central and Eastern Europe, including the countries of the FSU. The design and condition of Soviet-designed reactors was discussed by the Group of Seven (G7)[28] countries at their Munich Summit in July 1992, at which a Nuclear Safety Working Group was established. According to G7 analysis, of the 66 Soviet-designed reactors in operation across the region, only 35 were considered to be upgradeable in ways that would meet EU concerns about safety.[29] Those reactors that could not be upgraded should be closed as soon as possible. Nuclear safety initiatives have been aimed partly at persuading Russia to close reactors that are considered unsafe and to undertake refurbishment of the

---

[27] IAEA, Convention on Nuclear Safety, IAEA document INFCIRC/449, adopted at Vienna on 17 June 1994, URL <http://www.nti.org/db/nisprofs/fulltext/infcirc/safety/safetxt. htm>. The goal of the convention is to legally bind participating states that operate nuclear power plants to maintain a high level of safety. Parties must submit reports on the implementation of their obligations for peer review at meetings held at the IAEA.

[28] The G7 became the G8 at the Birmingham Summit in 1998. The Russian Federation will complete the process of becoming a full member at the 2006 Moscow Summit when it assumes the G8 Presidency for the first time.

[29] A study on nuclear safety issues in Eastern Europe was commissioned after the 1992 Munich Summit, which in turn led to the development of the 'G7 Action Plan on Nuclear Safety in Eastern Europe'. Okamura, Y., 'Achievements and experiences of Japan's programmes in Russia and the NIS', Paper presented to the Conference on the Non-Proliferation and Disarmament Cooperation Initiative, Brussels, 16–17 Dec. 2002.

remaining reactors to bring them up to international safety standards. In certain cases, if it can be agreed that a nuclear facility cannot be upgraded and should be closed, external economic and technical assistance may be applied to accelerate decommissioning while respecting agreed safety standards.

There have been different expert opinions about the quality of the designs used in Soviet reactors, and Russian authorities do not accept that their nuclear safety record is poor by international standards.[30] Russian authorities have resisted the closure of reactors. However, these projects have helped to develop and support a dialogue among national nuclear regulatory authorities and international organizations such as the European Atomic Energy Community (EAEC, Euratom) and the IAEA. The nuclear safety initiatives have also supported the development and conduct of nuclear safety training programmes based on agreed international standards and attended by Russian nuclear facility managers and employees.

In Europe, a narrow geographical focus on nuclear safety concerns in the FSU could not be justified because of the fairly large number of soviet-designed reactors in other countries. Very significant nuclear safety efforts have been undertaken in countries in Central and south-eastern Europe in addition to projects in Russia and the FSU.

European CTR efforts in northern Europe can be traced back to a speech by President Gorbachev in Murmansk in 1987 that seemed to offer the chance to develop a new kind of relationship with what was then the USSR.[31] Gorbachev pointed to the possibility that cooperative efforts among countries in northern Europe might solve common military and civilian problems within the sub-region. Gorbachev underlined the opportunities to address *inter alia* aspects of naval nuclear weapons and mutual concerns about environmental degradation. Countries in northern Europe, in particular Finland and Norway, saw in this speech an opening that could be used to initiate cooperation projects with Russia that could help to improve political relations as well as being valuable in and of themselves.

---

[30] Russian scientists consider the safety record of VVER type reactors, which were built in Central Europe, to be fully in line with international standards. Considerable safety improvements were made to RBMK type reactors (the type built at Chernobyl) after 1986.

[31] 'Mikhail Gorbachev's speech in Murmansk at the ceremonial meeting on the occasion of the presentation of the Order of Lenin and the Gold Star to the city of Murmansk', Murmansk, 1 Oct. 1987, archived at URL <http://projects.sipri.se/SAC/871001.html>.

Since the end of the cold war European countries have progressively established an institutional framework for cooperation to enhance environmental protection through the creation of sub-regional groupings in northern Europe. In September 1989, on the initiative of Finland, officials from eight countries (Canada, Denmark, Finland, Iceland, Norway, Sweden, the USA and the USSR) met to discuss cooperative measures to protect the Arctic environment. In 1991 these countries agreed an Arctic Environmental Protection Strategy that included a pledge to implement measures to control pollutants and reduce their adverse effects on the Arctic environment.[32] Subsequently, and in the framework of these decisions to cooperate on environmental protection, two new institutions for sub-regional cooperation—the Barents Euro-Arctic Council (BEAC) and the Council of Baltic Sea States (CBSS)—have conducted activities relevant to CTR.[33]

Since the accession of Finland and Sweden to the EU in 1995 efforts to enhance environmental protection in northern Europe have been increasingly EU-led. This tendency was strengthened when the EU adopted its Northern Dimension for external and cross-border policies in December 1998.[34]

In parallel with the development of a new institutional framework, informal cooperation among the states in northern Europe has continued to play a significant role in CTR. In particular, the trilateral cooperation that has been established between Norway, Russia and the USA in the Arctic Military Environmental Cooperation (AMEC) has led to the development and implementation of a number of projects.

Many of the priorities of the environmental protection programme have little to do with CTR as it has been defined in the past. The USSR pursued an extremely irresponsible policy with regard to nuclear environmental protection, routinely carrying out clandestine dumping of waste in unmarked locations.[35] However, Soviet behav-

---

[32] Documents relating to the Arctic Environmental Protection Strategy are available on the Internet site of the Arctic Council at URL <http://www.arctic-council.org/aeps.html>.

[33] See the organizations respective Internet sites at URL <http://www.beac.st>; and URL <http://www.cbss.st>. Their activities are discussed in chapter 2, section II of this report.

[34] See note 13.

[35] Russian analysts believe that the USSR acted in broadly the same manner as other countries in this respect. Prior to the signing of the Convention on the Prevention of Marine Pollution by Dumping of Wastes and Other Matters (the London Dumping Convention) on 29 Dec. 1972, Japan, the Netherlands, the UK and the USA are all believed to have dumped nuclear

iour was no better in relation to other items and substances that damage the environment. While a full 'mapping' of pollution and waste-related environmental problems is not possible, one of the primary objectives has been to understand the scale of the problem and its implications. In many cases these implications might not be directly related to human safety but might reflect, for example, the implications for commercial activities (such as fishing or tourism) of public concern about nuclear hazards, whatever the origin of these hazards might have been.

While addressing the environmental impact of military activities has not been the organizing principle for environmental cooperation projects, these activities could not be excluded because they have created serious concerns. The environmental protection measures have given a prominent place to projects that examine how to identify and then deal with spent nuclear fuel from the engines of decommissioned Russian nuclear-powered submarines and ice-breakers as well as projects to help store and treat a range of radioactive waste, including mixed and liquid waste.

It has been pointed out that north-western Russia probably contains the highest concentration of nuclear activity—and the most severe nuclear-related problems—in the world. This concentration is a direct consequence of the rapid militarization of the USSR, which included a major expansion in nuclear activities in the Kola Peninsula. Similarly, the development of Soviet military infrastructure and forces in the Far East created potential environmental as well as security challenges for Japan, including the identified leakage of radioactive materials into the Sea of Japan.

V. Cooperative threat reduction and counter-terrorism

After the terrorist attacks on the USA in September 2001 the imperative to prevent either states or non-state groups from acquiring WMD has been the dominant feature in statements by a number of major powers. There is a continued emphasis on the interconnection between proliferation and terrorism.

waste in ways that are inconsistent with the obligations later accepted under the convention. The USSR similarly ceased to dump high-level radioactive waste in the sea after it ratified the London Dumping Convention in 1975. Russia continued dumping low-level waste, but this is not prohibited by the convention and is a practice carried out by many states.

At their summit meeting in Evian, France, in early June 2003 the leaders of the G8 declared that 'the proliferation of weapons of mass destruction and their means of delivery poses a growing danger to us all. Together with the spread of international terrorism, it is the pre-eminent threat to international security'.[36] At the EU–US summit meeting at the end of June 2003 Konstandinos Simitis, the President of the European Council, Romano Prodi, the President of the European Commission, and US President George W. Bush underlined their common view that 'the proliferation of weapons of mass destruction and their delivery systems constitutes a major threat to international peace and security'.[37]

EU High Representative for the CFSP Javier Solana has noted that terrorists committed to maximum violence, the availability of WMD and the failure of state systems could together create a radical new threat to Europe. Mass-impact terrorism is identified as a strategic threat against which deterrence will fail because it

lacks the constraints of traditional terrorist organizations. These usually wish to win political support and therefore exercise some self-restraint; ultimately they may be ready to abandon violence for negotiation. The new terrorist movements seem willing to use unlimited violence and cause mass casualties. For this reason the idea of obtaining weapons of mass destruction is attractive to them.[38]

Consequently, Solana has identified the proliferation of WMD as 'the single most important threat to peace and security among nations' where 'the most frightening scenario is one in which terrorist groups acquire weapons of mass destruction'.[39]

Three types of concern over nuclear-related risks have been particularly prominent: (*a*) that nuclear material would be acquired that is not weapon-grade but that could nevertheless be used to construct a

---

[36] 'Non-proliferation of weapons of mass destruction: a G8 declaration', Evian Summit, 1–3 June 2003, URL <http://www.G8.fr/evian/english/navigation/2003_G8_summit/summit_documents/non_proliferation_of_weapons_of_mass_destruction_a_G8_declaration.html>.

[37] European Union in the US, 'Joint Statement: European Council President Konstandinos Simitis, European Commission President Romano Prodi and US President George W. Bush on the proliferation of weapons of mass destruction', EU–US Summit, Washington, DC, 25 June 2003, URL <http://www.eurunion.org/partner/summit/summit0306/WMDStatement.htm>.

[38] Solana, J., 'A secure Europe in a better world', Report submitted by the EU High Representative for the Common Foreign and Security Policy to the European Council, Thessaloniki, 20 June 2003, p. 4, available at URL <http://ue.eu.int/pressdata/EN/reports/76255.pdf>.

[39] Solana (note 38), p. 5.

nuclear explosive;[40] (b) that radiological materials would be acquired and used to cause a radiological hazard in a radiological dispersal device, or 'dirty bomb';[41] and (c) that an attack on a nuclear installation would cause a radiological hazard.

There is a risk that nuclear material that is not weapon-grade could be used to make a nuclear explosive. However, experts question whether this kind of nuclear explosive would be attractive to groups planning to carry out terrorist acts. The device would be large, and therefore difficult to transport in a concealed manner, and could have other characteristics that limit its utility. In particular, it might not explode in the proper manner and it might be difficult to store, handle or maintain in working condition for an extended period.[42]

As noted above, CTR can make a valuable but limited contribution to preventing the proliferation of NBC weapons under current conditions. Over time its most significant contribution may be helping to reduce the risk that radiological dispersal devices will be used to commit terrorist acts, although this will depend on the elaboration of new projects.

The increased focus on radiological dispersal devices is an example of the replacement of a cold war threat picture, in which the adversary and the likely means of attack were more easily identifiable, with a more complex threat mosaic. This change has been accompanied by an effort to identify societal vulnerabilities and put in place measures to reduce the likelihood that they can be exploited. According to this logic, if it is not possible to identify adversaries with confidence it might nevertheless be possible to make a technical assessment of tactics that any possible adversary might employ as part of a strategy of societal disruption. If a modern, advanced society can be massively

---

[40] According to the definitions used by the US National Intelligence Council, *weapon-usable* material is uranium enriched to 20% or more in the uranium-235 and uranium-233 isotopes and any plutonium containing less than 80% of the isotope plutonium-238. *Weapon-grade* material is uranium enriched to more than 90% uranium-235 or uranium-233 or plutonium-239 containing less than 6% plutonium-240.

[41] A radiological dispersal device has been defined as 'any device, including any weapon or equipment other than a nuclear explosive device, specifically designed to employ radioactive material by disseminating it to cause destruction, damage, or injury by means of the radiation produced by the decay of such material'. Ford, J. L., 'Radiological dispersal devices: assessing the transnational threat', *Strategic Forum*, Institute for National Strategic Studies, National Defense University, no. 136 (Mar. 1998), URL <http://www.ndu.edu/inss/strforum/SF136/forum136.html>.

[42] The author is grateful to Vitaly Fedchenko for these technical insights.

disrupted by non-military attacks then this is the type of attack against which countermeasures need to be prepared. Projects to enhance nuclear safety and security could assist in reducing these threats. Projects that strengthen the effectiveness of nuclear regulatory authorities, lead to a modernization of security systems at nuclear facilities, and generate information about the location and volume of fissile material and other radioactive materials can be seen to be helping to reduce certain types of threat. For example, in the light of concern about the misuse of radioactive sources, efforts are currently being made to identify radioactive sources that are vulnerable to theft or diversion from their intended use.

Measures to help ensure that the decommissioning of nuclear installations take not only environmental factors but also security-related factors into account can also help to counter the potential acquisition of dangerous materials by unauthorized end-users.

The international legal framework that could guide the development of CTR projects designed to help deny terrorists access to radiological materials is not well developed. The IAEA has taken a leading role in trying to develop a comprehensive and coherent approach to nuclear and radiological security.[43] However, at present this approach is not in place and where standards have been established it has been in national legislation. Establishing and strengthening effective standards and regulatory systems therefore take place on a voluntary basis and there is not full confidence that such an approach can sustain the process of improving national systems of control.

The text of a Joint Convention on the Safety of Spent Fuel Management and on the Safety of Radioactive Waste Management,[44] the first legal instrument to directly address these issues, was agreed in September 1997. However, although Russia signed the convention in 1999 it has yet to ratify it.

At present the international agreements that establish standards for nuclear safety and security lack provisions that take into account the

---

[43] In Mar. 2002 the IAEA Board of Governors agreed a Nuclear Security Plan of Activities. An overview of the implementation of this plan is available in 'Measures to strengthen international cooperation in nuclear, radiation and transport safety and waste management', Report to the Board of Governors, IAEA general conference document, GOV/2003/47-GC47/7, 4 Aug. 2003, available at URL <http://www.iaea.org/About/Policy/GC/GC47/Documents/gc47-7.pdf

[44] The convention entered into force on 18 June 2001. The text of the convention is available on the Internet site of the International Atomic Energy Agency at URL <http://www-rasanet.iaea.org/conventions/waste-jointconvention.htm#entry>.

possible use of radiological materials as a weapon. The 1980 Convention on the Physical Protection of Nuclear Material (CPPNM),[45] which entered into force in 1987, was established to reduce the risks that might arise from international transportation of nuclear materials. The CPPNM does not address the questions of domestic use, storage and transport of nuclear materials or the issue of protecting nuclear facilities from sabotage. The IAEA is currently considering how to amend and supplement the CPPNM to establish agreed standards for measures that would address these concerns.[46] At present the development of standards, as well as the regulations needed to translate these standards into practical procedures, is undertaken at the national level.

It is clear that CTR projects could support the implementation of agreed standards at the national level, in Russia and elsewhere. While projects to assist with securing military stockpiles have been difficult to develop because of the lack of progress in arms control, developing measures to address risks associated with radiological material in civilian facilities will probably not pose the same problems. The risk posed by unauthorized access to radiological materials is recognized first and foremost by Russian authorities, but also in the external donor community. Meanwhile, addressing issues in civilian facilities would not raise the same problems with information sharing and access to facilities that exist in the military establishment. Projects to help with the safe and secure management of fuel assemblies are one of the main priorities of CTR and it is likely that there will be an expansion in the scope of these activities to take in additional types of radiological material.

[45] The Convention on the Physical Protection of Nuclear Material is available at URL <http://www.unodc.org/unodc/terrorism_convention_nuclear_material.html>.

[46] In Aug. 2001 the IAEA Board of Governors endorsed 4 physical protection objectives and 12 principles to ensure the security of nuclear materials. 'Nuclear verification and security of material: physical protection objectives and fundamental principles', IAEA Board of Governors', IAEA document GOV/2001/41, 15 Aug. 2001, available at URL <www.iaea. or.at/worldatom/About/Policy/GC/GC45/Documents/gc45inf-14.pdf>. An IAEA expert group consisting of representatives from 43 countries as well as the European Commission has been meeting regularly since 2001 to discuss modifications to the CPPNM. Worldatom: frontpage news, 'Nuclear security regime: work continues on strengthening the International Conven-tion on Physical Protection of Nuclear Material', IAEA, 17 July 2002, URL <http//: www.iaea.org/worldatom/Press/News/NucSecurRegime.shtml>.

VI. Cooperative threat reduction: issues and problems

It is clear from the above that no single organizing principle for CTR, whether based on technological, geographical or institutional characteristics, is adequate. Identified CTR activities cannot be confined to the realm of military security because they have not been carried out only in Russia and they have included different constellations of partners within multilateral projects. Moreover, while US and European approaches may reflect something of a bias in favour of military and non-military security measures, respectively, there is no neat division in this respect. The USA has been an important partner in many soft security projects, while European countries have been central to CW-destruction projects.

Coalitions including states, international organizations, regional organizations, local and regional government, NGOs and private-sector industrial concerns have jointly implemented CTR activities in the past. Currently, CTR is on the agenda of a growing number of governments and international organizations, and the diverse range of projects that have been carried out is mirrored in the different arrangements under which cooperation has been organized and managed.

The lack of a clear organizing principle for CTR as well as the diversity of participants and lack of ownership could create a challenge to sustaining and implementing programmes. At the same time, attempting to develop coherence by bringing the activities under the umbrella of one organization or under the leadership of one country, while theoretically attractive, would be very difficult in practice.

The majority of CTR projects have been organized bilaterally between states, predominantly reflecting cooperation between Russia and the USA. They have developed close cooperation on security issues managed through intensive bilateral contacts at different levels and involving different agencies. The Bush Administration has sought to consolidate these contacts into a new strategic framework that has been described as 'a comprehensive strategy to enhance [US and Russian] security'.[47] In addition to frequent contact between the most

---

[47] Groombridge, M. A., 'US views on arms control', United Nations Department for Disarmament Affairs, *A Disarmament Agenda for the 21st Century*, DDA Occasional Papers no. 6 (Oct. 2002). Groombridge was the special assistant to John Bolton, Under Secretary for Arms Control and International Security, at the US Department of State. The Joint Declar-

senior political leaders, bilateral contact has often been conducted through joint commissions of different kinds and has most recently been supplemented through the creation of a new group, the Consultative Group on Strategic Issues, which is made up of the defence and foreign affairs ministers from both countries. The group meets annually and, between meetings, its activities are supported by a number of working groups.

The US Department of Energy (DOE) has also played a central role in CTR in Russia and in other countries and has well developed procedures for managing its relations with Russian partners. The DOE is mandated to reduce threats from nuclear weapons by preventing and limiting the development of nuclear weapons, reducing threats from nuclear weapons through protection, elimination or redirection of weapon-grade and weapon-usable materials, and reducing nuclear safety risks. This mandate has a domestic and an international component. The Deputy Administrator for Defense Nuclear Nonproliferation in the National Nuclear Security Administration, an agency created inside the DOE in 1999, has responsibility for managing the international programme.[48]

While the USA has by far the largest national capacity to contribute to CTR efforts, no single state (not even the most powerful) has the resources and authority required to define and carry out the full range of tasks needed. One critical element of the international cooperation that is needed to implement CTR projects will be the combination of efforts by the EU, Russia and the USA.

A central determinant of whether CTR can achieve its potential in helping to enhance security will be the extent to which the USA and European countries can develop what has been called 'a coordinated and complementary approach'.[49] However, CTR has played a relatively minor part in the transatlantic dialogue. One of the barriers to the development of a more meaningful transatlantic discussion has been the failure of the EU to develop a coherent strategy to address

ation on a New US–Russian Relationship was signed in Moscow on 24 May 2002 by President Bush and President Putin on the occasion of the signing of the SORT Treaty.

[48] The Department of Energy also plays a role in initiatives to reduce the risk that personnel with knowledge derived from participation in Soviet (now Russian) nuclear weapons programmes will contribute to illegal programmes elsewhere. Specifically, it administers the Nuclear Cities Initiative and the Initiative for Proliferation Prevention.

[49] Quille, G., 'A transatlantic approach to non-proliferation and disarmament?', *European Security Review*, no. 16 (Feb. 2003), pp. 6–8.

the threat posed by weapon proliferation. The EU is now trying to remedy this deficiency through the development of a strategy, the basic principles of which were agreed in June 2003. A priority Action Plan, the EU Action Plan Against Proliferation of Weapons of Mass Destruction, has been developed for immediate implementation, pending the finalization of the broader strategy.[50]

Although non-proliferation, international disarmament and arms transfers together form one element of EU–US cooperation under the New Transatlantic Agenda, adopted in 1995, the Action Plan that defines specific activities under the agenda mainly refers to cooperation in multilateral arms control processes where the approaches of the EU and the USA have diverged in recent years.[51] This divergence was partly addressed at the EU–US Summit in Washington in June 2003, where a Joint Statement on the Proliferation of Weapons of Mass Destruction included a commitment to work together to address a number of specific proliferation challenges.[52]

In the absence of deeper or more systematic discussion, cooperation between the EU and the USA has mainly rested, first, on the Expanded Threat Reduction Initiative (ETRI)[53] and, second, on the Nonproliferation and Disarmament Cooperation Initiative (NDCI).[54]

In 1999 the USA and the Netherlands each organized one ETRI meeting (in Brussels and the Hague, respectively) to discuss the need for intensified cooperation between the USA and the EU to reduce the risks of the proliferation of NBC weapons and NBC weapon-related materials and technologies. These meetings each lasted for one day

---

[50] Council of the European Union, Basic principles for an EU strategy against proliferation of weapons of mass destruction, 10 June 2003, Council document 10352/03; and Council of the European Union, Action plan for the implementation of basic principles for an EU Strategy against proliferation of weapons of mass destruction, 13 June 2003, Council document 10354/1/03.

[51] The New Transatlantic Agenda and the Joint EU–US Action Plan are reproduced at URL <http://europa.eu.int/comm/external_relations/us/intro/index.htm>.

[52] Joint Statement (note 37). The statement did not indicate how this positive EU–US cooperation would be carried out. Subsequent activities have largely taken the form of cooperation between the USA and individual European countries.

[53] President Bill Clinton proposed the Expanded Threat Reduction Initiative in Jan. 1999. It significantly increased funding for cooperation with Russian, Ukraine and other Newly Independent States (NIS) to prevent the proliferation of WMD and the materials to make them. See URL <http://clinton4.nara.gov>.

[54] US Department of State, 'Second Nonproliferation Conference focuses on cooperation needs: Brussels conference also looks at future challenges', International Information Programs, 23 Dec. 2002, URL <http://usinfo.state.gov/topical/pol/arms/02122302.htm>.

and consisted of short briefings by countries on their national programmes and budgets.

Under the NDCI the European Commission has organized and hosted two ad hoc conferences on non-proliferation and disarmament cooperation in Russia and the other Soviet successor states. These meetings took place in 2001 and 2002, and a further meeting is planned for 2004. They were longer than the ETRI meetings and included more detailed information exchanges. While no NDCI meeting took place in 2003, there was an inter-parliamentary conference organized by the European Commission to explain CTR to representatives of national parliaments in EU member states and to the European Parliament.

At these meetings officials from the EU member states, the USA and Canada had the opportunity to present their national CTR programmes and projects, including the budgetary aspects and any international assistance required for successful implementation. While useful, the NDCI cannot provide a basis for sustained engagement between the USA and the EU on issues related to CTR or on non-proliferation, arms control and disarmament.

The EU is also in the process of reviewing and upgrading its mechanisms for cooperation and dialogue with Russia, which are acknowledged to be weak in the realm of security. The development of a deeper EU–Russian–US triangular understanding should be facilitated by the creation of the G8 Global Partnership, in which all three countries participate along with other interested states.

Programme definition and coordination

The above discussion underlines that CTR is becoming progressively more broad in its scope and that it is seen less as a purely bilateral activity and more in the context of wider international cooperation.

It is also clear from the above discussion that there is no single harmonized approach to the role of CTR. The USA, European countries, Russia and other Soviet successor states have all seen CTR in slightly different terms. The various approaches have reflected differences in perspective about how to define security, how to identify threats and how to establish a threat hierarchy. Following September 2001 there has been convergence at a declaratory and, to an increasing extent, at an operational level in approaches to the definition of threats and also to the design and implementation of remedial measures. The development of CTR has also been affected by this convergence.

Issues related to how choices are made about which projects should be supported and in which locations, and the underlying reasons for these choices, are now being taken up for the first time in, for example, the EU and the G8.

The current CTR agenda includes projects undertaken for reasons related to non-proliferation, disarmament, nuclear safety and environmental protection. The issue of counter-terrorism has been added to this list. Even if, as seems likely, emphasis in future planning will be placed on preventing access to WMD by states or groups planning to carry out terrorist acts, other objectives cannot be discarded because they are central to projects that are already in an advanced stage.

Current choices have been dictated by pragmatism and in the short term the projects to be given priority—such as the decommissioning of Russian nuclear submarines, the disposition of fissile materials and the destruction of CW stockpiles—build on work that either is already well under way or has been planned in detail, and for which the requirements are well understood. However, these projects are not necessarily those that make the greatest contribution to preventing mass-impact terrorism.

If, in future, CTR does focus more resources on threats related to mass-impact terrorism, programme coverage might be expected to broaden still further. If the objective is to reduce societal vulnerabilities then there is no reason not to include other types of critical infrastructure. For example, CTR could logically include international cooperation to reduce the vulnerability of society in cases where the national power grid, the chemical industry or the information technology and telecommunications infrastructures are subject to attack. There is currently a requirement to evaluate CTR projects to ensure coherence, for example, by ensuring that projects to enhance environmental protection do not create a proliferation problem. In future, the issues of how to set priorities (not least in resource allocation) and ensure coherence are likely to become increasingly complicated.

The overall CTR effort will probably become both 'wider' and 'deeper'. First, there is a need for a wider geographical application of projects to tackle problems that are not restricted to Russia and the other countries of the FSU, for example, related to accounting for and protecting stocks of radiological materials. The US Nuclear Threat Initiative[55] has identified large quantities of HEU distributed to civilian reactors and other facilities in over 40 countries. While subject to safeguards to reduce the risk that this material would be used in nuclear weapon production, the organization raised concerns that much of this material was stored at 'inadequately guarded' sites.[56] In essence, there are two options regarding such sites—either to upgrade security or to remove dangerous materials from them. There have been at least four cases in which material has been removed from sites to more secure storage in another country.[57] Senator Richard Lugar, a key figure in the development of US assistance to the FSU, has made clear his view that activities of the kind associated with CTR need to be conducted in all countries with NBC weapon programmes.[58]

Second, there will have to be deeper engagement with Russia to address issues that have so far resisted efforts to develop cooperative approaches. One such issue concerns outstanding questions related to facilities within the Russian military establishment connected with the development of BW. Another such issue is whether it will be possible to gain reassurances about the number, status and security of Russian nuclear weapons that are not subject to arms control agreements in conditions where Russia and the USA do not appear to have any plans to negotiate new bilateral nuclear arms control agreements.

The tendency of groupings such as the G8 to consider how they might approach CTR collectively reflects the feeling that a collective approach might be more efficient as a form of organization than the alternative—a web of bilateral arrangements that could create

[55] Cable News Network founder Ted Turner and former Senator Sam Nunn founded the Nuclear Threat Initiative in Jan. 2001. It is supported by a pledge from Turner and other private contributions. Its mission is to strengthen global security by reducing the risk of use and preventing the spread of nuclear, biological and chemical weapons. See URL <http://www.nti.org/>.

[56] 'Proliferation threats facing the United States', Testimony of Charles B. Curtis, President, Nuclear Threat Initiative before the Senate Foreign Relations Committee, 19 Mar. 2003. Curtis was citing findings in Bunn, M., Wier, A. and Holdren, J. P., *Controlling Nuclear Warheads and Materials: A Report Card and Action Plan* (Nuclear Threat Initiative and the Project on Managing the Atom: Washington, DC, and Harvard, Conn., Mar. 2003), available at URL <http://www.nti.org/e_research/cnwm/overview/report.asp>.

[57] These cases were in Kazakhstan (Nov. 1994), Georgia (Apr. 1998), Serbia and Montenegro (Aug. 2002), and Romania (Sep. 2003).

[58] Lugar, R. G., 'NATO after 9/11: crisis or opportunity?', Speech to the Council on Foreign Relations, Washington, DC, 4 Mar. 2002, URL <http://www.acronym.org.uk/docs/0203/doc06.htm>.

unnecessary duplication. Other issues that are central to implementing the wider CTR programme might simply be impossible to resolve bilaterally—such as providing the technical, human or financial resources needed to facilitate a very large and complicated project.

Solutions to the problems raised in this chapter have clear implications for the organization of CTR, particularly in a European framework, given the work currently under way to further develop the conceptual and practical aspects of a CFSP to be applied by an enlarged EU. Some of the existing organizational forms for projects (such as European sub-regional cooperation) are not currently available in other locations. Considerable experience of implementing the kinds of projects envisaged by CTR has already been accumulated. The lessons from past experience in the political, legal and financial sphere need to be distilled to form the basis for future activities not only in Russia, but also elsewhere.

Against this background the remainder of this report addresses a number of questions. Chapter 2 examines and analyses the role that different types of threat reduction measures have played and currently play, including a discussion of the institutional setting in which they have been carried out. The G8 Global Partnership and the activities of the EU are important elements in the analysis. Chapter 3 examines project management and implementation more closely in an attempt to identify patterns of successful experience and the lessons learned from past experiences of CTR. Chapter 4 summarizes and draws conclusions.

2. The institutional framework for cooperative threat reduction

I. Introduction

The majority of the CTR projects that have been conducted have been designed and implemented on a bilateral basis. However, as chapter 1 made clear, the scale of the projects needed to achieve the objectives established for CTR is too large for any single country to carry the full burden of implementation. Moreover, it is likely that the scope of CTR will expand, both in terms of the number and size of projects undertaken in Russia and in geographical terms as projects are established in other countries.

The organization of projects in a manner that safeguards the interests of participating states while allowing efficient implementation and avoiding duplication, to the extent possible, is likely to require different approaches to be applied in different cases. There is not likely to be one single blueprint for CTR programme coordination. Where a project can be accomplished bilaterally there is no reason to make it unnecessarily complicated by involving other countries. However, even in cases of bilateral programmes, it is worthwhile to share information about the objectives and progress of projects and to describe the results of completed projects for a wider audience.

Given the multiple objectives discussed in chapter 1 for which CTR is pursued, there is a risk that many groups will be involved in implementing what are essentially the same projects and that this may detract from effective implementation.[59] That this could be a potential problem was one finding of a study led by the US Center for Strategic and International Studies, which highlighted that a number of countries with limited resources had been developing and implementing bilateral programmes, often without reference to each other.[60]

---

[59] Examples where this risk might already exist include projects for spent nuclear fuel storage, the development of safe and secure radioactive waste containers and submarine dismantlement.

[60] Einhorn, R. J. and Flournoy, M. A. (eds), Center for Strategic and International Studies (CSIS), *Protecting Against the Spread of Nuclear, Biological and Chemical Weapons: An action agenda for the Global Partnership,* vol. 3, *International Responses* (CSIS Press: Washington, DC, Jan. 2003), available at URL <http://www.csis.org/pubs/2003_future.htm>.

A variety of models can be identified from the programme coordination efforts that have been attempted. This chapter offers four case
studies that illustrate different types of international arrangements to
coordinate CTR. These case studies illustrate approaches to organizing programmes that could be applied to new types of problem and in
new locations.[61]

First, the CTR efforts of the EU are reviewed, which involve bilateral cooperation between the EU and other countries—most notably
Russia. (The EU itself is a unique arrangement involving intergovernmental cooperation among its member states and cooperation
between each of these states and the common institutions of the EU.)
Second, the Global Partnership organized by the G8 illustrates an
informal arrangement for intergovernmental cooperation. Third, the
International Science and Technology Center (ISTC) is an international organization based in Moscow in which the countries providing assistance and the countries receiving assistance are all parties
to the same legal agreement, which forms the statutory basis for the
centre. The fourth organizational case study illustrates intergovernmental cooperation within the framework of a treaty-based organization that is supported by specialized agencies. This case study
explores the experience of the United Nations and the North Atlantic
Treaty Organization (NATO), including their respective specialized
agencies.

None of the institutions or grouping arrangements covered here is
responsible for project implementation. Each, in essence, is attempting to set priorities and coordinate projects. One potential concern has
been that too many cooks might spoil the CTR broth. The chapter
concludes by comparing the case studies, considering their respective
advantages and disadvantages as forms for organizing CTR projects,
and examining whether there is currently duplication among the various coordination arrangements.

II. The European Union

The EU has recently begun to use the term CTR in its documents for
the first time. In 2003 the EU made CTR an important element within
its overall effort to develop a strategy against the proliferation of

---

[61] There are certain problems that seem unique to Russia, such as the existence of closed
nuclear cities. See Zarimpas (note 25), pp. 106–107.

WMD. This strategy is to be based on 10 'key elements', one of which is expanding CTR initiatives and assistance programmes.[62] One of the measures envisaged in the EU Action Plan to implement the strategy is an increase in EU CTR funding in the years beyond 2006.[63]

In the immediate future the experience that the EU gained from carrying out its assistance programmes in Russia will be invaluable and EU–Russian projects are likely to continue to be the main activities carried out. As the geographical and functional scope of CTR expands, the EU could play an important role in strengthening CTR in other places and through other types of project.

As part of its CFSP the EU is increasingly conscious of the need to develop a security strategy that takes into account a wide variety of threats. On 12 December 2003 a security strategy, drafted by the High Representative for the CFSP, was approved by EU member states.[64] This strategy should ensure the synergy noted above between policies pursued collectively by the EU and nationally by member states.

To implement new measures, the EU will need what has been called an 'effective multilateralism', that is, 'to be more active, more capable and more coherent in pursuit of common interests than has been the case in the past'.[65] One element of this effective multilateralism would be to evaluate all of the EU's external relations to determine where CTR measures could play a role and then discuss bilaterally which measures should be developed and how they should be implemented. To illustrate one potential means of carrying out such assessments, Javier Solana has pointed to the possible extension of the Common

[62] Council of the European Union, 'Basic principles for an EU strategy against proliferation of weapons of mass destruction', 13 June 2003, Council document 10352/1/03, pp. 4–5.

[63] Council of the European Union, 'Action plan for the implementation of the basic principles for an EU strategy against proliferation of weapons of mass destruction', 13 June 2003, Council document 10354/1/03, p. 6. The EU has established budget ceilings until 2006 for the different headings within the common budget, including budget headings from which increased funding for CTR would have to be taken. The budget process is discussed in Höhl, K. et al., *EU Cooperative Threat Reduction Activities in Russia*, Chaillot Paper no. 61 (EU Institute for Security Studies: Paris, 2003), p. 22, available at URL <http://www.iss-eu.org/chaillot/chai61e.pdf>.

[64] Solana, J., 'A secure Europe in a better world: the European Security Strategy', Approved by the European Council held in Brussels on 12 Dec. 2003 and drafted under the responsibilities of the EU High Representative Javier Solana, URL <http://ue.eu.int/solana/list.asp? BID=111>.

[65] Solana, J., Speech by the EU High Representative for Common Foreign and Security Policy to the Annual Conference of the Institute for Security Studies of the European Union, Paris, 30 June 2003, URL <http://ue.eu.int/solana/list.asp?bid=107&page=arch&archDate=2003&archMonth=6>.

Security and Defence Policy to include joint disarmament efforts supported by the EU.[66]

The development of the new security strategy is taking place against
the background of other transformations in the EU as it enlarges to
take in 10 new member states, prepares for further enlargement in the
future and adapts its institutions accordingly. This broad-based
approach means that attention will have to be paid to threats from
both inside and outside the boundaries of the enlarged EU as well as
threats from both military and non-military sources. Public statements
from EU officials have underlined that environmental and economic
concerns and the potential exploitation of weak or failed states by
organized crime and terrorism will continue to be taken into account
as part of the security strategy. The potential need for the EU to provide internal assistance to its member states as well as collective EU
assistance to other states will have to be part of an overall approach to
CTR.

The initiative to formulate a more coherent security strategy and the
agreements reached on stronger EU action against proliferation of
WMD are new developments. However, projects with characteristics
similar to those undertaken for CTR have a longer history within the
EU. As one group of authors has noted, this is an area where the EU
'has proved its ability to do useful work, and the division of labour
between the European Commission and the member states, despite all
the difficulties, has developed a positive synergy'.[67]

Cooperative threat reduction activity

The EU has carried out CTR-type activities for at least four separate
purposes and, as a result, different parts of the EU have taken responsibility for programme development.

The broad purposes of past assistance measures have been: (a) to
try to help Russia develop into a prosperous, well-governed and
environmentally sound state with which the EU can cooperate; (b) to
reduce the potential damage caused to the natural and human

---

[66] Solana (note 65). The idea is included in the first article defining the Common Security
and Defence Policy. Draft Treaty Establishing a Constitution for Europe, adopted by consensus by the European Convention on 13 June and 10 July 2003, European Convention Secretariat, CONV 850/03, Brussels, 18 July 2003, URL <http://europa.eu.int/futurum/
constitution/index_en.htm>.

[67] Höhl et al. (note 63), p. 50.

environment by developments in Russia; (c) to improve nuclear safety; and (d) to strengthen multilateral non-proliferation and arms control agreements.

While there have also been some relevant activities in other countries, most projects intended to meet these objectives have involved cooperation with Russia. Responsibility for defining and managing projects which have been initiated at different times has rested with different parts of the EU, and the pattern of activities has both reflected and been influenced by the key background developments in European security. Of these the most important have been the creation, in 1991, of the EU from the former European Communities and its subsequent evolution and enlargement to take in a state (Finland) that borders Russia, as well as the development of relations between this evolving EU and other states and organizations.

European CTR efforts in northern Europe formed part of the wider effort to develop a more constructive relationship with Russia after the end of the cold war. From the outset, these efforts to improve relations included a strong environmental security component, with nuclear-related issues being particularly prominent.

Environmental security cooperation

As noted above, Soviet President Mikhail Gorbachev's speech in Murmansk in 1987 pointed to the possibility for cooperative efforts among countries of northern Europe to solve common military and civilian problems within the sub-region.[68] These countries—in particular Finland and Norway—sought to use this opening to improve political relations with Russia and as the discussion of sub-regional cooperation extended to include the Baltic states, Estonia, Latvia and Lithuania, Swedish interest in participation also increased. At this time Finland and Sweden were not members of the EU. They joined the EU in 1995 but Norway is not a member.

In 1994 Norway, Russia and the USA set up the Murmansk Trilateral Initiative to improve the efficiency and effectiveness of the treatment of liquid nuclear waste from nuclear-powered ice-breakers at a treatment plant in Murmansk and to adapt the plant to treat waste from nuclear submarines. In 1996 Norway proposed the trilateral

---

[68] See note 31.

AMEC programme to focus on the problem of spent fuel from nuclear submarines.[69] The UK joined the AMEC programme in 2003.

The sub-regional cooperation between the Nordic countries and Russia in areas of soft security developed along many different paths and was institutionalized in a number of new arrangements. These sub-regional arrangements developed agendas covering a very broad spectrum. Nuclear safety and environmental protection have been prominent issues in several of them.

The CBSS, founded in 1992 as a forum for intergovernmental cooperation on a wide range of issues, includes 11 countries (Denmark, Estonia, Finland, Germany, Iceland, Latvia, Lithuania, Norway, Poland, Russia and Sweden) as well as the European Commission. One of the first actions of the CBSS was to establish the Working Group on Nuclear and Radiation Safety. One of its main activities was to collect information on sources of radioactivity in order to identify potential risks that require immediate remedial action. The working group was then asked to prepare and develop initiatives, based on this information, to address the problems identified. It became a forum in which bilateral projects and assistance to enhance nuclear security could be defined and developed. These projects were mainly bilateral, with the nuclear regulatory authorities in Finland and Sweden playing a particularly important role in cooperation with Russia and the Baltic states.[70] However, bilateral projects could also report their progress back to the working group and discuss any outstanding difficulties.

The BEAC was established in 1993 as a forum for intergovernmental cooperation on issues concerning the Barents Region. It has seven members (Denmark, Finland, Iceland, Norway, Russia, Sweden and the European Commission) and one of its first decisions was to develop an Arctic Environment Protection Strategy (known as the 'Rovaniemi process') supported by an expert task force. The BEAC has emphasized the need to find a safe means of managing nuclear waste, and the Rovaniemi process has provided a forum in which nuclear environmental projects have been organized and financed.

[69] The triangular Norway–Russia–USA cooperation is discussed in Krupnick (note 12), pp. 144–53.

[70] The Radiation and Nuclear Safety Authority in Finland (STUK) has been particularly active in developing cooperation with the Russian national nuclear regulatory authority, GAN, as well as in projects at the Leningrad and Kola nuclear power plants. The Swedish national authority, SKI, has also been active in projects together with the Leningrad power plant and at the nuclear power plant in Ignalina, Lithuania. Finland and Sweden have both sponsored nuclear waste management projects in Russia.

These projects aim to improve environmental monitoring and the sharing of information derived from that monitoring to identify problems created by radioactive materials as early as possible.

The BEAC also provided the initial forum in which the Multilateral Nuclear Environmental Programme in the Russian Federation (MNEPR) was discussed. The MNEPR Framework Agreement (discussed further below) provides a legal framework to guide states in drawing up specific documents establishing rules for the carrying out of particular projects related to the management of spent nuclear fuel and radioactive waste. The negotiation of the MNEPR started at the BEAC meeting in Bodø, Norway, in 1999 but the final obstacles to the agreed text were not removed until the BEAC meeting in Kirkenes, Norway, in January 2003. Subsequently, 11 countries as well as the European Community and Euratom signed the MNEPR Framework Agreement in Stockholm on 21 May 2003.[71]

The CBSS and the BEAC provided a framework for intergovernmental cooperation. They both included the European Commission as a participant. Since 1991 the European Commission has also provided grant-financed technical assistance to 13 countries on the territory of the FSU (through its Technical Assistance for the Commonwealth of Independent States, TACIS, programme) and 10 countries in Central Europe (through its Phare programme)[72] to help these countries replace their command economies and state socialist political systems. While the specific projects financed through TACIS and Phare have been tailored to the needs of each recipient, environmental protection and nuclear safety have been prominent elements in the overall programme of assistance.[73]

[71] The text of the Framework Agreement on a Multilateral Nuclear Environmental Programme in the Russian Federation (MNEPR) is available at URL <http://www.ud.se/inenglish/frontpage/MNEPR.htm>. The Framework Agreement was ratified by the Russian Duma on 10 Dec. 2003 and signed into law by President Putin on 27 Dec. 2003. It will enter into force 30 days after ratification instruments are received from Russia and from one other signatory and remain in force for a period of 5 years from that date. The signatories to the MNEPR Framework Agreement are Belgium, Denmark, Finland, France, Germany, the Netherlands, Norway, Russia, Sweden, the UK and the USA as well as the European Community and Euratom.

[72] The Phare programme is 1 of 3 pre-accession instruments financed by the EU to assist the applicant countries of Central Europe with their preparations for joining the EU. Originally created to assist Hungary and Poland, it later included all 10 candidate countries of Central and Eastern Europe. See URL <http://europa.eu.int/comm/enlargement/pas/phare/>.

[73] E.g., TACIS-financed projects include investigating potential sites in Russia for nuclear waste management plants, evaluating waste management plant designs, assessing spent

Following the 1986 Chernobyl accident European countries sought to raise the level of safety at nuclear installations in Central and Eastern Europe. This work was also supported by specific projects financed by the Phare and TACIS assistance programmes. The European Commission carries out activities intended to enhance nuclear safety through the CONCERT Group, which was formed in 1992 to bring together nuclear regulators from Central Europe, Eastern Europe and the EU to consider issues of common concern—including nuclear safety and nuclear waste management.[74]

Approaches to technical assistance and procedures for project implementation will have to change in preparation for the enlargement of the EU to 24 nations in May 2004. Although the Central European countries joining the EU have a national responsibility to make certain that they implement the commitments in agreements to which they are party, it remains the case that a number of candidate countries still face economic difficulties in taking all of the steps necessary to satisfy these commitments. The EU cannot manage relations with its member states using instruments developed for foreign assistance. However, there is a strong incentive to assist new member states to implement their national safety and security-related commitments under international agreements after they join the EU because these countries will participate in the single market and be part of the Schengen area, which facilitate the movement of items and people throughout the EU.

The European Commission implements a large number of nuclear-related research programmes. Since 1997, the EU has carried out separate bilateral cooperation with Russia in the field of joint research on nuclear safety. In 2001 this cooperation was strengthened under a bilateral agreement that *inter alia* envisages cooperation in the field of nuclear waste management, nuclear safeguards and nuclear material accountancy.[75]

---

nuclear fuel transport requirements and undertaking regional waste management studies in the Murmansk and Archangelsk regions. In addition to the TACIS programme, the European Commission Directorate on the Environment has also sponsored studies on interim storage facilities for spent nuclear fuel and has financed the development of prototype containers for nuclear fuel. See URL <http://europa.eu.int/comm/external_relations/ceeca/tacis/>.

[74] Background documents relating to the CONCERT Group are available at URL <http://europa.eu.int/comm/energy/nuclear/safety/concert_en.htm>.

[75] 'Agreement for cooperation between the European Atomic Energy Community and the Government of the Russian Federation in the field of nuclear safety', 30 Oct. 2001, *Official Journal of the European Communities*, L287 (31 Oct. 2001), pp. 24–29.

In 1997, Finland's Prime Minister Paavo Lipponen proposed the creation of a 'northern dimension' to EU policies with a view to engaging the EU more deeply in actions across a wide range of areas. Established in December 1998, intensive discussions during the Finnish presidency of the EU, in 1999, led to the adoption of the Northern Dimension Action Plan in June 2000.[76] In the course of 2001, environmental issues came to be seen as perhaps the main priority for the Northern Dimension, and the elaboration of a Northern Dimension Environmental Partnership (NDEP) is its most tangible achievement.[77]

The NDEP was developed to address the problem of how to finance Northern Dimension environmental projects in the absence of any separate funding line within the EU common budget. Addressing the environmental problems identified in north-western Russia (that part of Russia falling within the Northern Dimension area) required projects that are too large and too expensive to be financed from existing national sources or from the existing budgets established by international financial institutions or the European Commission. The NDEP has tried to meet this funding requirement by establishing a steering group and a support fund. The steering group consists of international financial institutions—the European Bank for Reconstruction and Development, the European Investment Bank, the Nordic Investment Bank and the World Bank—as well as the European Commission and the Russian Government. The support fund is a joint account into which donors can pay financial contributions.[78] The European Commission is the primary contributor to the account while Denmark, Finland, Germany, the Netherlands, Norway, Russia and Sweden have all made contributions.

Under the NDEP arrangement a lead bank is designated to manage the financial aspects of priority projects agreed by the steering group.

---

[76] Council of the European Union, Action Plan for the Northern Dimension with external and cross-border policies of the European Union 2000–2003, Brussels, 14 June 2000, URL <http://europa.eu.int/comm/external_relations/north_dim/ndap/06_00_en.pdf>.

[77] One evaluation has concluded that 'one specific area within the Northern Dimension policy umbrella that has recently moved forward in very practical terms is the Northern Dimension Environmental Partnership'. Sigurdsson, J., 'Environmental safety and regional cooperation in the Barents region', Presentation to the Conference on Murmansk and New Possibilities in the Barents Region, Murmansk, 24 Jan. 2003.

[78] Background documents on the Northern Dimension Environmental Partnershsip and its support fund are available at URL <http://europa.eu.int/comm/external_relations/north_dim/ndep/index.htm#back>.

The lead bank puts together a financial package consisting of a mix of loans (provided from its own resources and from steering group partners) and grants (from the resources of the support fund).

One of the priority projects identified by NDEP is the Kola Peninsula nuclear waste clean-up project. The overall cost of this project (which is actually a catalogue of potential projects to manage spent nuclear fuel as well as solid and liquid nuclear waste) is estimated to be €500 million and, as of early 2003, €62 million had been pledged to the NDEP support fund to meet the needs of the project.

While the NDEP focuses on financing, the other central element of the Northern Dimension Action Plan that is relevant to CTR is the MNEPR Framework Agreement, referred to above, along with its accompanying Protocol on Claims, Legal Proceedings and Indemnification.[79]

The MNEPR Framework Agreement provides an agreed set of rules that any of the signatories can take advantage of when designing projects for implementation in Russia in the areas of enhancing the safety of spent nuclear fuel and nuclear waste management. It should facilitate interactions between project participants in order to resolve disagreements related to project implementation, if they arise. It establishes rules for the disclosure of financial information and the verification of project-related spending as well as exemptions from customs duties and taxation in connection with financial and technical contributions to projects covered by the agreement.

The Protocol to the Framework Agreement establishes rules covering issues of liability in case project implementation leads to damage of various kinds. The projects envisaged deal with hazardous materials and will be carried out in locations where geographical conditions and the climate can be severe. There is, therefore, a risk of loss of life, personal injury and loss of or damage to property during the completion of a project. The project participants have insisted on understanding what the extent of their liability would be in such cases including the rules for compensation, making good economic losses

---

[79] Council Decision of 19 May 2003 on the signing on behalf of the European Community and provisional application of a Framework Agreement on Agreement on a Multilateral Nuclear Environmental Programme in the Russian Federation [MNEPR] and its Protocol on Claims, Legal Proceedings and Indemnification and approving the conclusion by the Commission on behalf of the European Atomic Energy Community of the abovementioned Agreement and its Protocol, 2003/462/EC, *Official Journal of the European Union*, L 155 (24 June 2003), pp. 35–46. The text of the protocol is available at URL <http://www.ud.se/inenglish/frontpage/MNEPR.htm>.

arising out of damage caused and the costs of both preventive and remedial damage limitation measures during project implementation. Article 8 of the MNEPR Framework Agreement covers the use and re-transfer of items provided during the implementation of a project. It commits parties not to divert or re-transfer items for any purposes other than those agreed in the context of the specific project being carried out. It also commits Russian authorities to take 'all reasonable measures' in their power to ensure that the terms of this article are respected. The article, which underlines Russian responsibilities to prevent the diversion or unauthorized re-export of items received in connection with CTR projects, is intended to simplify export licence assessments in donor countries.

The Framework Agreement established an MNEPR Committee composed of one authorized representative from each of the signatories. This individual is also designated as the point of contact for all questions of relevance to the MNEPR. The European Commission signed the MNEPR Framework Agreement on behalf of the EU and it represents the EU on the MNEPR Committee. National representatives of the eight EU member states that signed the MNEPR (Belgium, Denmark, Finland, France, Germany, the Netherlands, Sweden and the UK) also sit on the committee and there is a requirement for the European Commission to coordinate its position with these member states prior to committee meetings.

With the NDEP and the MNEPR signed and in place, it is expected that a number of projects which have been under discussion for several years will now be implemented. In particular, fairly rapid progress is expected on projects related to nuclear submarine decommissioning and storage of spent nuclear fuel.

Non-proliferation and disarmament cooperation

The EU began to carry out specific and targeted CTR activities much later than it initiated environmental security cooperation. In December 1999 it adopted the Joint Action Establishing a European Union Cooperation Programme for Non-proliferation and Disarmament in the Russian Federation.[80]

---

[80] Council Joint Action, 17 Dec. 1999, Establishing a European Union Cooperation Programme for Non-proliferation and Disarmament in the Russian Federation, 1999/878/CFSP, URL <http://www.eur.ru/eng/neweur/user_eng.php?func=rae_disarmament>.

To an extent, this reflects the specific character of the EU and its institutions. The European Commission was able to take the initiatives described above in the area of environmental protection and nuclear safety because these issues fall within its legal competence. Consequently, the Commission is able to propose legislation, develop projects and provide financing for these areas of activity. By contrast, arms control is regarded by member states as an aspect of security policy. Placing any given issue within this realm has, in the past, taken it beyond the purview of the European Commission and made it a question to be addressed intergovernmentally under the auspices of the Council of the European Union—made up of representatives from the member states.

The content of the CFSP was discussed during the Intergovernmental Conference that preceded the entry into force of the 1993 Treaty on European Union (Maastricht Treaty). Arms control, non-proliferation, the control of arms exports, and confidence- and security-building measures were all elements that were considered appropriate subjects for the CFSP. After 1993 the scale and importance of initiatives in arms control, non-proliferation and disarmament grew progressively within the EU and initiatives were taken across the spectrum of NBC and conventional weapons. While the list of activities of different kinds undertaken by the EU is fairly long, on inspection it can be seen that actions in the area of NBC weapons, in particular, have been limited in their scope and duration if compared either to activities in the environmental area or projects carried out at the national level by EU member states, especially France and Germany.[81]

In the past, EU institutional arrangements have been perceived as a barrier to effective action. Any member state with different views on an issue from its partners could block the consensus needed for a decision on a particular project. The actions of the Commission could also be blocked if a member state suspected that it was exceeding or trying to expand its jurisdiction. Under these conditions it has been easier for many member states to keep decision making and project manage-

---

[81] The most comprehensive description of European national contributions to CTR is contained in Einhorn and Flournoy (note 60). By contrast, the EU acted both more often and more substantively in areas related to conventional arms. Anthony, I., 'European Union approaches to arms control, non-proliferation and disarmament', *SIPRI Yearbook 2001: Armaments, Disarmament and International Security* (Oxford University Press: Oxford, 2001), pp. 599–614.

ment under exclusively national control. Bilateral cooperation has largely been the preferred form with Russia.

In line with the greater maturity of the EU in general, the different parts of the EU have learned how to organize more effective action. Moreover, the EU is preparing new decision-making mechanisms that should reduce the barriers to cooperative action still further.[82]

The 1999 Joint Action established financial support for a project to destroy CW at a plant in Gorny as well as facilitating studies on plutonium transportation, storage and disposition. In 2001 the scope of the Joint Action was expanded to include the provision of financial assistance to help construct the CW destruction facility at Shchuchye in Russia.[83] The 1999 Joint Action was time-limited and expired in June 2003. At that time a new decision was taken to prolong the activities.[84]

The renewal of the Joint Action in 2003 underlines the continuing role for EU engagement in Russia, although an opportunity was missed to expand the scope of activities. The Joint Action envisages a key role for the Commission in preparing projects and supervising their implementation. To carry out its responsibilities, the EU maintains an expert unit in Brussels and a project assistance team in Moscow. It had been hoped that the new Joint Action would establish and finance new projects in Russia in the areas related to bio-safety and security as well as export control cooperation and that the Commission would be used to oversee and manage these projects. In the event, this did not happen and the Joint Action remains limited to projects in the important areas of fissile material disposition and CW destruction.

The decision to continue the Joint Action was accompanied by budget preparations within the Commission in anticipation of an expanded programme that is likely to be put in place after 2006. The

---

[82] E.g., the Draft Treaty Establishing a Constitution for Europe would, if adopted, create a European External Representative who would chair a newly created EU Foreign Affairs Council and also serve as vice-president of the European Commission. Draft Treaty (note 66).

[83] Report to the European Council on the Implementation of the Common Strategy of the European Union on Russia, Council document 9805/1, 12 June 2001; and European Council, Presidency Conclusions, Gothenburg, 15–16 June 2001, URL <http://www.eu2001se/static/pdf/eusummit/conclusions_eng.pdf>.

[84] Council Joint Action, 24 June 2003, On the Continuation of the European Union Cooperative Programme for Non-proliferation and Disarmament in the Russian Federation, 2003/472/CFSP, *Official Journal of the European Union*, L 157 (26 June 2003), pp. 69–71.

programming of the budget for the period 2004–2006 was agreed before the issue of non-proliferation came to the fore and the governments of EU member states have not been prepared to revise their plans, which have been heavily influenced by the need to support the costs of enlarging the EU to take in new members. However, if nuclear reactor safety-related activities are excluded from the definition of the Global Partnership a significant increase in funding for CTR may be required during the period 2007–12 to reach the level of €1 billion in financial support pledged by the EU to the Global Partnership.[85]

In addition to its internal reviews of future cooperation within the framework of the Joint Action, the EU will also have additional possibilities to review progress on CTR together with Russia within the framework of an enhanced EU–Russian political dialogue.

The EU concluded a Partnership and Cooperation Agreement with Russia that entered into force in December 1997[86] and a Common Strategy on Russia that was adopted in June 1999.[87] These documents have together provided the framework for EU–Russian cooperation. In 1999, the Common Strategy between the EU and Russia emphasized the need for cooperation to meet identified 'common challenges on the European continent' including efforts to promote a clean environment and measures to ensure nuclear safety and the safe handling of nuclear waste. As noted above, these priorities were subsequently followed up with specific projects.

The EU is currently in the process of reviewing the mechanisms for cooperation and dialogue with Russia, which are acknowledged to be weak in the realm of security. While the Common Strategy on Russia was renewed without modification in the summer of 2003, it has been recognized by both Russia and the EU that reinforced cooperation would be desirable. At their St Petersburg Summit in May 2003 the EU and Russia issued a joint statement describing their intention to

---

[85] Nuclear reactor safety projects are financed through the TACIS programme and through the International Science and Technology Center in Russia and the Science and Technology Center in Ukraine. Between 2004 and 2006, around €450 million will be provided in this manner. Including these figures would mean that the EU would meet its Global Partnership spending commitment without any increase in its contribution to weapon non-proliferation.

[86] The Partnership and Cooperation Agreement between the EU and Russia is available at URL <http://europa.eu.int/comm/external_relations/ceeca/pca/index.htm>.

[87] The Common Strategy between the European Union and Russia, *Official Journal of the European Communities*, L 157 (24 June 1999), p. 1, URL <http://europa.eu.int/comm/external_relations/ceeca/com_strat/index.htm>.

replace the existing Cooperation Council with a new council to act as a clearing house for all issues of EU–Russia cooperation. The Permanent Partnership Council is intended to meet more frequently than the Cooperation Council did and in different formats, and it should be supported by sufficient resources to permit thorough preparation and coordination on both sides. Non-proliferation of WMD, their means of delivery and related technology is specifically identified as one area that needs greater EU–Russian cooperation. The Permanent Partnership Council has a review function, including regular reports on the Russian capacity to absorb and utilize EU assistance. This review will include both specific independent evaluations and audits of particular projects.[88]

While the institutional framework has been created for a significant expansion of EU–Russia cooperation in the area of non-proliferation, no decisions have been taken to follow through and create a programme comparable to the existing cooperation on nuclear reactor safety. There is still no document or programme that lays out a common, substantive EU–Russian security agenda beyond the statement that multilateral agreements should be strengthened. Moreover, this last statement could be interpreted as a common defensive goal in the face of certain tendencies in US policy that raise misgivings in both Europe and Russia, as much as the basis for a common set of active measures to strengthen multilateral processes.

III. The Global Partnership Against the Spread of Weapons and Materials of Mass Destruction

The Heads of State and Government of the G8 countries announced the creation of the Global Partnership Against the Spread of Weapons and Materials of Mass Destruction in June 2002.

The G8 does not have a secretariat. The country holding the chair is responsible for hosting and organizing the annual G8 summit meetings. The annual summit meeting is the principal G8 activity that brings together the leaders for talks on issues considered to be of

[88] EU–Russia Summit: Joint Statement, 31 May 2003, document no. 9937/03 (Presse 154), URL <ue.eu.int/pressData/en/er/75969.pdf>. In this document the EU and Russia have also committed themselves to work together in the multilateral framework in order to strengthen the disarmament, arms control and non-proliferation regimes and to promote their universalization.

global importance to the group. In advance of the meeting the host country organizes meetings between personal representatives of the leaders to set the agenda. The G8 host country is not responsible for implementing commitments made at the summit meeting (beyond its own national commitments) or for monitoring implementation. However, the host country usually organizes inter-summit meetings of a network of senior officials, who focus on the major issues on the agenda. As a general rule, the chair has also taken on the responsibility for engaging non-G8 countries, NGOs and international organizations in discussions relevant to the issues on the agenda. Given the characteristics of the G8, observers have questioned how effective it would be in coordinating activities to avoid duplication with other efforts, how well it could facilitate the effective implementation of key projects and whether it could sustain the momentum necessary for a programme undertaken over the 10-year period envisaged in the Global Partnership.

While the G8 process involves a political commitment at the highest level, in the past it has placed a low emphasis on coordination and ensuring coherent national implementation of its political commitments. This is partly because its apparatus, while keeping costs low and flexibility high, does not permit the development of specialist knowledge of issues raised, or maintain close ties with national agencies responsible for implementing commitments made at the meetings.

From as far back as the July 1990 Houston Summit the Heads of State and Government of the G7 have made statements about the urgent need to address the threat from transnational terrorism and the proliferation of NBC weapons.[89] At the 1992 Munich Summit the G7 agreed that they would support the FSU in efforts to ensure that nuclear materials from dismantled nuclear weapons would not be returned to military use. However, it has not been possible to identify the precise role of the G7/G8 in developing measures to tackle these issues.

At their 1996 Moscow Nuclear Safety and Security Summit the G7 made a commitment to achieve a high standard of safety in the use of nuclear power worldwide. Kenneth Luongo has pointed out that the

---

[89] G7 Heads of State or Government, Statement on transnational issues and terrorism, Houston Summit, 10 July 1990, available at URL <http://www.ioc.u-tokyo.ac.jp/~worldjpn/documents/texts/summit/19900710.D2E.html>.

Box 2.1. The G8 Global Partnership: principles to prevent terrorists, or those that harbour them, from gaining access to weapons or materials of mass destruction

The G8 calls on all countries to join them in commitment to the following six principles to prevent terrorists or those that harbour them from acquiring or developing nuclear, chemical, radiological and biological weapons, missiles and related materials, equipment and technology.

1. Promote the adoption, universalization, full implementation and, where necessary, strengthening of multilateral treaties and other international instruments whose aim is to prevent the proliferation or illicit acquisition of such items; strengthen the institutions designed to implement these instruments.

2. Develop and maintain appropriate effective measures to account for and secure such items in production, use, storage and domestic and international transport; provide assistance to states lacking sufficient resources to account for and secure these items.

3. Develop and maintain appropriate effective physical protection measures applied to facilities which house such items, including defence in depth; provide assistance to states lacking sufficient resources to protect their facilities.

4. Develop and maintain effective border controls, law enforcement efforts and international cooperation to detect, deter and interdict in cases of illicit trafficking in such items, for example, through installation of detection systems, training of customs and law enforcement personnel and cooperation in tracking these items; provide assistance to states lacking sufficient expertise or resources to strengthen their capacity to detect, deter and interdict in cases of illicit trafficking in these items.

5. Develop, review and maintain effective national export and transshipment controls over items on multilateral export control lists, as well as items that are not identified on such lists but which may nevertheless contribute to the development, production or use of nuclear, chemical and biological weapons and missiles, with particular consideration of end-user, catch-all and brokering aspects; provide assistance to states lacking the legal and regulatory infrastructure, implementation experience and/or resources to develop their export and transshipment control systems in this regard.

6. Adopt and strengthen efforts to manage and dispose of stocks of fissile materials designated as no longer required for defence purposes, eliminate all CW, and minimize holdings of dangerous biological pathogens and toxins, based on the recognition that the threat of terrorist acquisition is reduced as the overall quantity of such items is reduced.

Source: Statement by G8 leaders, 'The Global Partnership Against the Spread of Weapons and Materials of Mass Destruction', Kananaskis, Canada, 27 June 2002, available at URL <http://www.g8.gc.ca/2002Kananaskis/kananaskis/globpart-en.asp>.

commitments made in 1996, related to nuclear safety, nuclear material safety (including preventing illicit trafficking in nuclear materials), nuclear waste management, and nuclear material control, accountancy and physical protection, were not subsequently translated into specific activities.[90]

At the 1998 Birmingham Summit the G8 leaders also made a commitment to enhance their cooperation on the effective implementation of export controls. However, before 2003, few specific ideas on how to implement export controls or make them more effective can be traced to the G8.[91]

The original Global Partnership statement included two elements: a set of six principles to prevent terrorists, or those that harbour them, from gaining access to weapons or materials of mass destruction (box 2.1) and a set of guidelines for new or expanded cooperation projects to translate these principles into practical activities (box 2.2).

The principles should have an impact on the internal activities of the G8 countries. They apply to nuclear weapons, BW defence programmes, fissile material stocks no longer required for defence purposes, radiological source materials and missile infrastructures in all the G8 countries. Moreover, through the participation of the EU, the principles now apply to 15 European countries and in future will apply to the 25 member states of the enlarged EU. The G8 Global Partnership and these six principles contributed to the political momentum that led to the increased efforts by the EU to develop its strategy against WMD proliferation.

As well as making them the basis for their own policies the G8 countries agreed to work to embed the six agreed principles into the agreements of other groups and organizations in which they participate. On 20 January 2003, at the ministerial-level meeting of the UN Security Council on combating terrorism, the foreign ministers of the G8 countries stressed the importance of actions to prevent terrorists from gaining access to weapons or materials of mass destruction. Sev-

---

[90] The need for new or expanded cooperation projects to address nuclear safety issues is one element of the guidelines agreed by the G8 states in the Global Partnership, which established a Nuclear Safety and Security Group to address implementation of past commitments. Luongo, K. N., 'Perspectives on the G8 Global Partnership Against the Spread of Weapons of Mass Destruction', Testimony before the Senate Committee on Foreign Relations, Washington, DC, 9 Oct. 2002, URL <http://www.ransac.orgl>. Kenneth N. Luongo is Executive Director of the Russian–American Nuclear Security Advisory Council.

[91] It should be acknowledged, however, that in 1987 it was the G7 countries that formed the initial membership of the MTCR.

Box 2.2. The G8 Global Partnership: guidelines for new or expanded Cooperation Projects

The G8 will work in partnership, bilaterally and multilaterally, to develop, coordinate, implement and finance, according to their respective means, new or expanded cooperation projects to address (1) non-proliferation, (2) disarmament, (3) counter-terrorism and (4) nuclear safety (including environmental) issues, with a view to enhancing strategic stability, consonant with our international security objectives and in support of the multilateral non-proliferation regimes. Each country has primary responsibility for implementing its non-proliferation, disarmament, counter-terrorism and nuclear safety obligations and requirements and commits its full cooperation within the Partnership.

Cooperation projects under this initiative will be decided and implemented, taking into account international obligations and domestic laws of participating partners, within appropriate bilateral and multilateral legal frameworks that should, as necessary, include the following elements:

1. Mutually agreed effective monitoring, auditing and transparency measures and procedures will be required in order to ensure that cooperative activities meet agreed objectives (including irreversibility as necessary), to confirm work performance, to account for the funds expended and to provide for adequate access for donor representatives to work sites;
2. The projects will be implemented in an environmentally sound manner and will maintain the highest appropriate level of safety;
3. Clearly defined milestones will be developed for each project, including the option of suspending or terminating a project if the milestones are not met;
4. The material, equipment, technology, services and expertise provided will be solely for peaceful purposes and, unless otherwise agreed, will be used only for the purposes of implementing the projects and will not be transferred. Adequate measures of physical protection will also be applied to prevent theft or sabotage;
5. All governments will take necessary steps to ensure that the support provided will be considered free technical assistance and will be exempt from taxes, duties, levies and other charges;
6. Procurement of goods and services will be conducted in accordance with open international practices to the extent possible, consistent with national security requirements;
7. All governments will take necessary steps to ensure that adequate liability protections from claims related to the cooperation will be provided for donor countries and their personnel and contractors;
8. Appropriate privileges and immunities will be provided for government donor representatives working on cooperation projects; and
9. Measures will be put in place to ensure effective protection of sensitive information and intellectual property.

Source: Statement by G8 leaders, 'The Global Partnership Against the Spread of Weapons and Materials of Mass Destruction', Kananaskis, Canada, 27 June 2002, available at URL <http://www.g8.gc.ca/2002Kananaskis/kananaskis/globpart-en.asp>.

eral of the ministers stated that these actions include denial of such weapons and materials to states known to have supported groups that carry out terrorist acts. One attempt to achieve this was the introduction of ideas contained in the G8 statement into the UN Security Council discussions on combating terrorism. The agreed guidelines have almost certainly facilitated the signing of legal agreements to set the rules for bilateral or multilateral government-to-government assistance programmes with Russia. As noted above, while agreement on a Declaration of Principles on a Multilateral Nuclear Environmental Programme in the Russian Federation was reached in March 1999, it proved impossible to translate this declaration into a legal Framework Agreement until May 2003. After the 2002 Kananaskis Summit the senior officials responsible for developing the Global Partnership made reaching agreement on the MNEPR Framework Agreement one of their priorities. While no direct link can be traced from the actions of the G8 to the signing of the agreement, which may well have been influenced by a number of factors, these discussions undoubtedly helped.

The second important element of the Global Partnership established at the Kananaskis Summit were guidelines to be applied to CTR projects. Given the characteristics of the G8 noted above, the participating states do not see it as an executive body. However, because of the very wide range of projects that could theoretically fall within the scope of the Global Partnership, it has proved necessary to consider how the G8 should meet their identified responsibilities.

After the Kananaskis Summit a group of G8 officials reviewed outstanding issues in existing negotiations related to bilateral and multilateral agreements required for projects falling under the scope of the Global Partnership. Starting from the premise that the G8 should not duplicate existing bilateral and multilateral structures for project implementation, the conclusion reached was that at present the G8 could make its most effective contribution by focusing high-level political attention in order to help identify and remove obstacles to the implementation of projects.

To this end, it was agreed that a Senior Officials Group should be officially constituted and that it must be composed of individuals with sufficient seniority and decision-making authority to resolve many questions without the need for further discussions.[92] The chair of the group (which meets frequently, often on a monthly basis) should be a high official from the country currently chairing the G8.[93]

After June 2002 the Senior Officials Group focused on four main objectives: (*a*) translating the guidelines into concrete actions and implementing legal agreements; (*b*) initiating and developing specific projects; (*c*) monitoring the national implementation of the commitment to raise up to $20 billion over the next 10 years; and (*d*) beginning outreach activities to expand participation in the Global Partnership. The G8 has also established an annual review mechanism that leads to the preparation of an annual report presented to the Heads of State and Government at their annual summit meeting. The first annual report was presented at the Evian Summit in June 2003.[94]

Following the 2002 Kananaskis Summit a question remained over which projects would be subject to the agreed guidelines. It appears that no detailed catalogue of projects has been compiled. Moreover, defining and funding specific projects that fall under the programme of work and then implementing these projects is the responsibility of the participating states. However, in their annual report, the Senior Officials Group identified a number of projects where progress had been made during the preceding year.

1. Construction of the CW destruction facility at Gorny had been completed and it had commenced operation.

2. There had been agreement to construct a CW destruction facility in the town of Kambarka, in the Russian Republic of Udmurtia.

3. Construction of the CW destruction facility for nerve agents at Shchuchye had commenced, along with related infrastructure projects.

[92] Maerli Bremer, M. and Anthony, I. (eds), *Conference Proceedings from the 2003 G8 Pre-Summit Seminar on Strengthening Cooperative Threat Reduction in the Northern Region*, (SIPRI and the Norwegian Institute of International Affairs, NUPI: Stockholm, May 2003), available at URL <http://projects.sipri.se/nuclear/pre_proc.pdf>.

[93] Anin, A., 'Global'noe partnerstvd protiv rasprostraneniya oruzhiya i materialov massovogo unichtozheniya: god proshel, chto dal'she?' [Global Partnership Against the Spread of Weapons and Materials of Mass Destruction: a year has passed, what next?] undated article, available at URL <http://www.pircenter.org/data/gp/anin.pdf>. Anatoly Anin is believed to be a pseudonym for Ambassador-at-large Anatoly Antonov, Russian representative to the Senior Officials Group.

[94] G8 Senior Officials Group Annual Report, presented at the Annual Summit of the G8 Heads of State and Government, Evian, June 2003, URL <http://www.g8/fr/evian_report.html>.

4. There had been progress with projects to dismantle nuclear submarines in the north-western and far-eastern regions of Russia, and with the funding of other projects for the dismantlement of decommissioned nuclear submarines.

5. Agreement had been reached on a programme to end Russian production of weapon-grade plutonium and on the acceleration of efforts to secure Russian fissile material and nuclear warheads.

6. Significant progress had been made with negotiations on international support for Russia's plutonium disposition programmes, including increased financial pledges, as well as substantial agreement on effective programme management and oversight.

7. Progress had been made with improving the safety and security of biological research facilities.

8. Efforts were continuing in the ISTC to provide employment for former weapon scientists.

9. New bilateral engagements had been initiated with former non-conventional weapon production facilities to assist with their conversion to develop and manufacture commercial products.

In its working procedures the Senior Officials Group has left the initiative to Russia to identify specific projects and propose them to partners. On the basis of their analysis of the list presented by the Russian side, partners may respond individually to any of the ideas it contains.[95] However, in the Global Partnership's initial phase, priority is being given to projects that conform to the priorities identified at Kananaskis (destruction of CW, dismantlement of decommissioned nuclear submarines, disposition of fissile materials and employment of former weapon scientists). Within this list Russia has placed special emphasis on the destruction of CW and the dismantlement of decommissioned submarines.

In January 2003 the Russian Ministry for Atomic Energy (MINATOM) sent several nuclear submarine dismantlement project proposals related to submarines located in different parts of Russia to G8 partners. During 2003 Canada, Germany, Japan, Norway and the UK all began the process of allocating the funds needed to begin decommissioning projects. In an interview in October 2003, Deputy Minister Sergey Antipov provided an update of the current status of discussions, noting that 'as far as multi-purpose submarines are concerned, the only state with which the agreement on dismantlement of two submarines has been concluded is Norway. There is no real result with any other state, although there are some substantial developments with Japan, Germany and the United Kingdom'.[96]

While the Global Partnership is likely to include other countries in the future, Russia—a full participant in the G8 from 2006—will be treated differently from other countries facing demilitarization challenges. In Russia, CTR cooperation is to be carried out on a full partnership basis. It may be the case that in other countries the approach will contain elements of conditionality.[97]

Since the adoption of the Global Partnership only countries considered to be fully committed to the G8 principles to prevent terrorists, or those that harbour them, from gaining access to weapons or materials of mass destruction are eligible for assistance from the G8 states. This may act as an incentive to states requiring assistance to ensure that they are compliant. However, the G8 states have a strong self-interest in the implementation of CTR projects. It will therefore be interesting to see how G8 countries interpret this particular element of the Global Partnership.

The G8 principles include a commitment to fully implement multilateral treaties that contribute to effective non-proliferation as well as a commitment to enforce national export controls. In Russia questions about arms control compliance and suspicions about the effectiveness of export controls were a barrier to CTR project implementation in the past. However, these issues have now been decoupled and, while concerns remain about Russian activities in certain regards, these will not prevent CTR assistance from being supplied in future.

By the time the G8 Heads of State and Government met in Evian, France, one year after the decision to establish the Global Partnership the G8 Senior Officials Group responsible for monitoring its implementation had identified specific and confirmed pledges amounting to $18 billion. Moreover, the Senior Officials Group pointed out that, in the short term, the participating states had made adequate provision in

---

[96] 'Utilizatsiya APL: finishnoi lentochki poka ne peresek nikto' [Nuclear submarine dismantlement: nobody has reached the finish yet], undated interview with Russian Federation Deputy Minister for Atomic Energy Sergey Antipov, available at URL <http://www.pircenter.org/data/gp/int_Antipov.pdf>.

[97] It should be noted that Russian analysts are doubtful about whether the USA will eliminate elements of conditionality from its assistance programmes.

their national budgets for 2003–2004 to meet their identified spending commitments.[98] The annual report of the Senior Officials Group is an important transparency measure given the risk that donor countries might otherwise question the fulfilment of financial pledges made at Kananaskis and afterwards. The annual report could, in future, also play a useful role in enhancing domestic support for CTR in donor countries. However, this would require the publication of additional and more detailed information on financial contributions than that contained in the first report.

The pledge of a financial contribution, which represents a political commitment by the current government in each of the respective countries, does not mean that all of the resources pledged over the lifetime of the Global Partnership are firmly anchored in the budget plans of the contributors. However, in comparison with the total resources allocated to the kinds of activities envisaged by the Global Partnership in the past, this level of expenditure will represent a very significant increase for some G8 countries, should it be achieved.

A comparison of the financial data in table 2.1 (future spending commitments) with those in table 2.2 (the pattern of past spending) illustrates the scale of the individual increases, and the collective increase in spending that will be needed if EU countries are to meet their commitments under the Global Partnership. In comparison with the 10-year period for fiscal years 1992/93–2001/2002, total EU spending will have to increase by a factor of 12 between 2002 and 2011 from approximately €400 million to over €5 billion. As stated above, most of this increase will probably occur after 2006.

While, at Kananaskis, the G8 leaders stated that the initial focus of the Global Partnership would be projects in Russia, it was also envisaged that the Global Partnership would extend to other countries. The G8 has subsequently stated that it would be willing to enter into negotiations with any other recipient countries prepared to adopt its guidelines with a view to including them in the partnership. In 2003 Ukraine presented an official application for consideration by the G8 to which the Senior Officials Group responded positively in principle. During 2003 more informal contacts also took place between the Senior Officials Group and representatives of Kazakhstan.

Whereas projects to assist Russia were initially conceived according to a donor–recipient principle, the Global Partnership has been put

[98] G8 Senior Officials Group Annual Report (note 94).

Table 2.1. Maximum national commitments[a] by Global Partnership
participants over the 10-year period 2002–2011.

Partner	Original currency	US dollars[b] (million)
Canada	CAN$1 billion	637
EU	€1 billion	941
France	€750 million	706
Germany	€1.5 billion	1412
Italy	€1 billion	941
Japan	US$200 million	200
Russia	US$2 billion	2000
UK	€750 million	706
USA	US$10 billion	10 000

[a] Participants at the 2002 Kananaskis G8 Summit committed themselves to raise
amounts 'up to' these figures.
[b] Using the International Monetary Fund average market exchange rate for 2002.

Source: G8 Senior Officials Group Annual Report presented at the Annual Summit
of the G8 Heads of State and Government, Evian, France, June 2003.

forward on a different basis. This is also reflected in the procedures of
the G8 in that Russia participates fully in all discussions and is a party
to all decisions. The fact that Russia has pledged to spend the equivalent of $2 billion on projects agreed to fall within the Global Partner-
ship in 2002–12 played an important role in creating this partnership
principle. Moreover, Russia has followed through on its commitment
by contributing roughly $205 million from its 2003 budget to Global
Partnership activities and will match this spending in the budget for
2004. While the principle of partnership applies within the G8 discussions, project implementation will continue to take place on a
bilateral or multilateral basis and will involve the provision of financial, material and technological support from seven of the G8 states,
together with the EU, to the eighth participating state—Russia.[99]

[99] After the G8 Evian Summit, President Putin stated that Russia would also be prepared
to contribute to the implementation of the Global Partnership in other countries. Russia could
contribute either financially or by making available the technical and human resources developed during the implementation of CTR projects in Russia. Zayavleniya dla pressy po okon-
chanii sammita [Comments to the press after the G8 summit], *Bolshoi vosmerki*, Official
Internet site of the President of the Russian Federation, 27 June 2002, available at URL
<http://president.kremlin.ru/text/appears/2002/06/29029.shtml>.

As the G8 expands its geographical focus, this hybrid arrangement in which Russia is both a partner (and therefore a financial contributor) and a recipient of assistance will not, as the Global Partnership is currently conceived, exist with other countries. As noted above, the generation of new projects is likely to depend on lists submitted by potential recipients of assistance. Russia currently participates in the Senior Officials Group to discuss its own submission and will also have a voice in the discussion of future project proposals submitted by other states. Given the scale of the projects required in Russia and the urgency of the tasks, there could be a natural tendency on the part of Russia to promote its national interests at the expense of those of other potential recipients of assistance. This situation will require the G8 to maintain a policy of transparency to reassure countries such as Kazakhstan and Ukraine that they are being treated fairly in comparison with Russia.

To help meet the challenge of raising up to $20 billion, the G8 have stated that 'recognizing that the Global Partnership is designed to enhance international security and safety, the G8 invites others to contribute to and join in this initiative'.[100] All states that can subscribe to the Kananaskis guidelines, are willing to adhere to the six principles for assistance and have ongoing CTR work with Russia or FSU states are, in principle, welcome to join what has been called the *extended partnership*.

After June 2002 the G8 organized a number of meetings with interested countries. There is no minimum financial commitment required for participation in the extended partnership. While there is no intention to modify the G8 itself, at the 2003 Evian Summit the Global Partnership was broadened to non-G8 countries when Finland, Norway, Poland, Sweden and Switzerland stated their intention to participate.[101] The flexibility of the G8 means that there is no difficulty in including senior officials from countries that meet the criteria for participation in the extended partnership although they are not members of the G8.

In addition to developing its cooperation with non-G8 contributors and non-Russian recipients of assistance, it will be necessary to ensure coherence between the G8 Global Partnership and other G8 efforts.

---

[100] Statement by G8 leaders (note 4).

[101] 'Actions at the G8 summit: day two', The White House, Office of the Press Secretary, Washington, DC, fact sheet, 2 June 2003, URL <http://www.state.gov/e/eb/rls/fs/21153.htm>.

Table 2.2. Summary of European Union financial contributions, fiscal years 1992/93–2001/2002
All figures are in millions of euros.

Source	Committed	Estimated spend
EU Joint Action	15.5	12.0
TACIS	196.0	184.0
Finland	2.0	1.5
France	147.0	77.0
Germany	72.8	70.5
Italy	44.1	6.1
Netherlands	14.0	2.3
Sweden	11.6	10.8
UK	113.7	4.8
Total	**616.7**	**369.0**

Source: Defrennes, M., Paper presented to the Conference on the Non-proliferation and Disarmament Cooperation Initiative, Brussels, 16–17 Dec. 2002.

To ensure coherence between the different efforts in the field of nuclear safety and security, the G8 agreed to establish a new Nuclear Safety and Security Group before the Evian Summit. At Evian the G8 attempted to give a strong political impetus to efforts by the IAEA to enhance protection against nuclear terrorism.[102] It issued an Action Plan intended, first, to support the work of the IAEA in the area of nuclear safety and security and, second, to work for a political commitment from the roughly 100 states judged by the IAEA to lack the legislative and regulatory framework needed to control radioactive sources adequately.

The G8 countries will need to develop cooperation with non-G8 contributors as well as non-Russian recipients of assistance. However, it is also necessary for the G8 to try to ensure coherence between different G8 efforts. While the Senior Officials Group is responsible for the Global Partnership, the G8 has a number of other working groups in which officials come together to discuss issues related to aspects of the Global Partnership.

A Nonproliferation Group has met for a number of years to discuss developments in the multilateral arms control treaties. A Nuclear

---

[102] These efforts are discussed further below.

Safety and Security Group was established before the Evian Summit, at which the G8 tried to give strong political impetus to efforts by the IAEA to enhance protection against nuclear terrorism. At Evian the G8 issued a Statement and launched an Action Plan on Securing Radioactive Sources.[103] The Action Plan pledges to increase G8 support to the IAEA Nuclear Safety Fund and to take responsibility for organizing a conference in 2005 to review the progress of IAEA efforts.

G8 officials also meet in a Counter-terrorism Group, which has developed proposals to strengthen joint efforts to curb terrorist threats to mass transport.[104] As noted above, at the 1998 Birmingham Summit the G8 leaders agreed to take steps to enhance the effectiveness of export controls. At the same meeting the G8 leaders also noted that man-portable air defence weapons (MANPADS) were a serious threat to civil aviation. MANPADS are mainly surface-to-air missiles small enough to be fired from the shoulder or from a small stand. In 2003 the G8 participating states agreed a number of measures to help control MANPADS (of which there are a large number in the inventories of military forces across the world) more effectively.

The portability of these weapons, and their potential effectiveness against large and slow aircraft such as civilian airliners, is thought to create a significant risk of terrorist acquisition and use.[105] At their meeting in Evian the G8 leaders called on countries to strengthen control over their national stockpiles of MANPADS. Leaders agreed on a number of steps to assist with this strengthening of control, including the provision of assistance and technical expertise to help with the collection, secure storage and stockpile management of MANPADS as well as the destruction of any weapons considered to be surplus.[106] This decision has extended the application of CTR from weapons and

---

[103] Non Proliferation of Weapons of Mass Destruction, Securing Radioactive Sources: A G8 Statement; and Non-proliferation of Weapons of Mass Destruction, Securing Radioactive Sources: A G8 Action Plan. available at URL <http://www.g8.fr/evian/english/navigation/2003_g8_summit/summit_documents.html>.

[104] Information on G8 activities is available at the G8 Information Centre Internet site, URL <http://www.g7.utoronto.ca>.

[105] There have been a significant number of cases of actual or attempted use of such weapons against civilian aircraft. Moreover, for Russia, the use of these weapons by opposition fighters in Chechnya has led to the loss of significant numbers of helicopters and fixed-wing military aircraft.

[106] Enhance Transport, Security and Control of Man-portable Air Defence Systems (MANPADS): A G8 Action Plan, available at URL <http://www.g8.fr/evian/english/navigation/2003_g8_summit/summit_documents.html>.

materials of mass destruction to one category of conventional weapons.

The G8 working groups are not organized in a hierarchical manner and officials from different agencies meet in the various working groups. The Senior Officials Group consists of high-level officials that report directly to the offices of the G8 leaders while the other working groups consist of technical specialists who report to their respective ministries or agencies. The manner and extent to which representatives on the different working groups coordinate their work at the national level and the ways in which the working groups interact will probably have to be reviewed as the Global Partnership develops.

Looking forward, the G8 Heads of State and Government agreed six objectives at their 2003 summit meeting that the USA, which holds the rotating presidency of the G8 until June 2004, will try to advance. The Action Plan objectives are in essence a statement of continuity in that, as described above, most of them have already been the focus of attention from the Senior Officials Group.

The identified objectives are: (*a*) to pursue the universal adoption of the non-proliferation principles; (*b*) to reach the Kananaskis commitment of raising up to $20 billion over 10 years through contributions from new donors or additional pledges from existing partners;[107] (*c*) to significantly expand project activities, building on preparatory work to establish implementing frameworks; (*d*) to develop plans for project activities and sustain steady progress in projects already under way; (*e*) to resolve all outstanding implementation challenges and to review the implementation of all guidelines in practice; (*f*) to expand participation in the Global Partnership to interested non-G8 donor countries that are willing to adopt the Kananaskis documents; (*g*) to maintain the focus on projects in Russia but also enter into preliminary discussions with new or current recipient countries that are prepared to adopt the Kananaskis documents; and (*h*) to publicize the importance of the Global Partnership to other organizations, parliamentary representatives and the general public.

---

[107] Among the G8 partners there are different interpretations of the Kananaskis commitment. While the USA believes that the Russian contribution of $2 billion is in addition to the $20 billion pledged under the Global Partnership, other G8 partners believe that the Russian contribution forms part of the commitment.

In some public statements the Russian Government has emphasized the need to accelerate project implementation and an impatience can be detected regarding the pace at which the G8 partners are moving forward at the national level.[108]

In summary, as a statement of intent from the highest level of government, the G8 Global Partnership reflects the political impetus behind both non-proliferation and counter-terrorism. However, it raises a number of substantive questions about its scope and definition as well as a number of institutional questions related to the management and administration of whatever programme can be defined.

Whether the G8 process can or will succeed in developing and implementing a work programme and sustaining it over an extended period of time is still to be tested. However, in a short space of time the Global Partnership has already emerged as an important element within a wider set of interlocking measures being pursued by states and other actors with a view to eliminating or controlling threats to their security. Moreover, the G8 countries have taken steps to increase the effectiveness of their cooperation.

The specific projects that will be in focus in the initial stages of the Global Partnership appear to be the destruction of CW stockpiles, the decommissioning of nuclear submarines and nuclear waste clean-up in north-western Russia. These are urgent tasks because of the risks posed to the natural environment in Russia and beyond but they make a modest contribution to non-proliferation and counter-terrorism. In order to reduce the risks of mass-impact terrorism, however, other activities will be needed in Russia and projects will need to be carried out in countries other than Russia. With the adoption of the measures related to MANPADS as well as those related to nuclear terrorism, the G8 is further expanding the technical scope of its activities regarding practical measures to identify, secure and destroy weapons and materials of great current concern in respect of counter-terrorism.

IV. The International Science and Technology Center

In 1992 the EU, Japan, Russia and the USA established the International Science and Technology Center as an international organiza-

---

[108] Kalinina, N., Remarks to the Second Carnegie International Nonproliferation Conference, Moscow, 19 Sep. 2003. Natalya Kalinina is Assistant to the Prime Minister of the Russian Federation,

tion to help prevent the proliferation of technologies and expertise related to NBC weapons. In order to develop its enormous military, technical and industrial capacities the USSR had trained a huge number of scientists, technicians and production workers. In the critical economic and social conditions prevailing after the break-up of the USSR it was important to ensure that these human resources were supported and assisted to find peaceful occupations.

This was intended to be a temporary expedient because, in the early 1990s, the scientific and industrial base that supported the defence sector was considered to be the most capable and advanced part of the Soviet economy. It was believed that those individuals and enterprises from this sector who were no longer supported by Russian military spending would be able to find commercially viable non-military employment. A temporary mechanism was needed to provide weapon scientists and engineers with alternative employment in order to reduce the incentives that they would have to put their skills to unauthorized uses.

To meet this requirement the ISTC was established in November 1992 through an international agreement.[109] Under the agreement the ISTC consists of a Governing Board made up of representatives from the EU, Japan, Russia and the USA. In addition, one seat on the board is occupied on a rotational basis by countries located on the territory of the FSU that have become parties to the agreement. There are 11 parties to the ISTC Agreement: Russia, the USA and the EU (the founding parties); Armenia, Belarus, Georgia, Kazakhstan, Kyrgyzstan and, since 2003, Tajikistan (the Commonwealth of Independent States, CIS, parties); and Norway and the Republic of Korea (other parties).

The Governing Board approves new parties, sets funding criteria and decides which projects to fund on behalf of the ISTC. The ISTC has a Coordination Committee on which all parties to the agreement are represented equally. This committee is primarily charged with overseeing project implementation. The Coordination Committee works closely with the Secretariat, which is responsible for the day-to-day operation of the ISTC. In addition, all parties select and designate

---

[109] Agreement establishing an International Science and Technology Center, 27 Nov. 1992. The agreement is available on the ISTC Internet site at URL <http://www.istc.ru/istc/website.nsf/fm/z01AgreementE>.

participants to a Scientific Advisory Board on the basis of their technical expertise in areas where the ISTC carries out projects. The ISTC main office is in Moscow, and branch offices have been established in Armenia, Belarus, Georgia, Kazakhstan and Kyrgyzstan.

The centre functions as a clearing house for scientific and technical projects generated by Russian individuals and establishments. Through the ISTC these entities can publicize their activities and seek partners.[110] The ISTC maintains databases of projects and researchers and can help to establish cooperation through electronic communications, supporting the costs of international travel by Russian entity representatives, and organizing and financing seminars with foreign partners.

The ISTC can also offer practical assistance. The centre evaluates proposals from the Russian side and can suggest modifications based on recommendations either from its Scientific Advisory Committee or from its international staff. The centre offers patent support, helping Russian entities to secure international patents for ideas and inventions with potential commercial applications created in ISTC-sponsored projects. It is also a source of project funding—both by using its own resources and by helping projects to find financial support from governments, intergovernmental organizations or NGOs that support its work.

A recent assessment of the ISTC highlights its success measured in terms of the number of scientists and projects that have been supported by ISTC-sponsored activities.[111] The legal agreement that established the ISTC also specified its status under Russian law and has conferred a number of rights and responsibilities on the centre itself and the projects carried out under its auspices. This agreement included *inter alia* rights related to taxes and currency movements associated with ISTC activities, access to locations and information connected with projects and the settlement of any legal claims arising out of ISTC activities. The ISTC can establish bank accounts in Russia, including for individuals that work in the closed nuclear cities

---

[110] In Dec. 2001 the ISTC Commonwealth of Independent States Technology Portal went online. It contains an enormous amount of information about individuals, projects and technologies in the FSU, much of it available in searchable databases. The portal can be accessed at URL <http://www.tech-db.ru/ISTC/DB/techdb.nsf/NSHomeEng?ReadForm>.

[111] Alessi, V., 'The brain drain problem', eds R. J. Einhorn and M A Flournoy, Center for Strategic and International Studies (CSIS) *Protecting Against the Spread of Nuclear, Biological and Chemical Weapons: An action agenda for the Global Partnership*, vol. 2, *The Challenges* (CSIS: Washington, DC, 2003), pp. 23–52.

that made up the Soviet nuclear weapon complex. Probably for this reason, an external observer has pointed out that the ISTC projects, once approved, seem 'immune from many of the day-to-day irritations that plague other Russian programs. Difficulties are usually resolved quickly and amicably'.[112]

At the same time, some of the assumptions underlying the original decision to establish such a centre have proved questionable. The Russian defence sector was expected to reorient itself towards non-military activities and the demand for the activities of the ISTC, and their cost, was expected to decline as Russian entities increasingly operated on a commercial basis.

The ISTC has tried to make itself 'an efficient tool for matching the needs of world industry with relevant expertise in Russia and the CIS'.[113] While it did make a great deal of information available about science and technology in the FSU, it is difficult to evaluate the role of the ISTC in establishing commercial activities in Russia or the other countries where regional offices are located. However, there appears to be increasing agreement that the commercialization of technology developed by former weapon scientists and engineers may not remain the main emphasis of the ISTC.

Younger engineers no longer choose a career in the Russian nuclear weapon establishment and many chose to leave during the 1990s if the opportunity presented itself. One recent US study has suggested that the ISTC might have an important role to play by using its research financing to support projects that, in effect, provide a pension supplement for an ageing Russian nuclear workforce that cannot otherwise afford to retire.[114] The natural reduction in the numbers of scientific and industrial nuclear specialists to a point where the size of this workforce matches the needs of maintaining Russia's nuclear force structure will take approximately 20 years. In 2002 the Governing Board of the ISTC, far from phasing out its activities, moved to make it a more permanent organization.

Tajikistan became a party to the ISTC Agreement in 2003. Norway and the Republic of Korea have been parties to the ISTC Agreement

[112] Alessi (note 111), p. 9.

[113] International Science and Technology Center, Annual Report 2002, URL <www.ostc. ru/ISTC/sc.insf/htmc/annual-report.html>.

[114] Weiner, S. K., 'Preventing nuclear entrepreneurship in Russia's nuclear cities', *International Security*, vol. 27, no. 2 (fall 2002), p. 152.

since 1992 and at least one additional country (Canada) has expressed an interest in joining. The Governing Board has restated the need for activities to continue while at the same time discussing how a transition could be made to a full partnership approach. This would include the removal of any residual 'donor–recipient' characteristics in project evaluation and implementation, in part through the recruitment of Chief Science Coordinators (international staff selected only against criteria of technical expertise) to promote and coordinate ISTC inputs to projects. The new approach would also emphasize the internationalization of activities (e.g., through the creation of international science laboratories).

The ISTC has tried to emphasize projects that not only assist workers from the defence sector in general, but also focus in particular on those who possess the most critical knowledge and skills related to the development and production of WMD or missile delivery systems. However, it has not been possible to evaluate the success of the ISTC projects in the Russian Federation in achieving this objective.

V. Other international organizations

While perhaps not usually thought of as CTR, there are other initiatives that have some of the same basic characteristics as the processes described above. Moreover, these types of initiative may come to play a more important role as the scope of CTR begins to expand in an effort to destroy or place under closer control a broader range of items that may be used to commit acts of mass-impact terrorism.

The United Nations

The IAEA, is an independent agency that is part of the United Nations system. It has played a critical role in establishing parts of the framework in which CTR projects have been carried out. One of its main functions is to develop nuclear safety standards and it has a mandate to provide for the application of these standards. Agreements made under the auspices of the IAEA have established key objectives and standards for nuclear safety that CTR projects have, in turn, tried to help states to achieve.

In 1999 a group of experts presented recommendations to the IAEA Board of Governors intended to strengthen the regulations on nuclear security to reduce the risk that radioactive materials would be stolen. In September 2001 the IAEA General Conference endorsed these recommendations by adopting a set of Physical Protection Objectives and Fundamental Principles.[115] At the same time, the IAEA established a new expert group to draft amendments to the 1980 Convention on the Physical Protection of Nuclear Material that would translate these guidelines into an international legal agreement.

In March 2002 the IAEA agreed a plan of action to protect against nuclear terrorism based on an evaluation of possible radiological threats and a classification of which radiation sources would be the most desirable from the perspective of terrorists.[116] The plan includes recommended standards for nuclear material accountancy and control systems and procedures. In addition, many of the physical protection recommendations that have been included are 'guards, guns and gates' measures of a type that have in the past been undertaken, in Russia in particular, as part of CTR projects.[117]

The IAEA regularly reviews and updates a range of nuclear regulations of different kinds. Since 2001 these reviews have included consideration of how the various regulations might be altered to take into account current concerns. One of the main activities has been to consider how to identify so-called 'orphan' radiological sources— sources that have not been disposed of but which are no longer under the control and supervision of national regulatory authorities.

While the IAEA has developed a great deal of technical knowledge about how to help recover radiation sources, it has limited capacities to assist member states relative to the number of known problems. The individual IAEA member states are responsible for ensuring that agreed standards are implemented and the agency is taking on additional projects to provide advice and training to member states on request. One proposal is to expand the range of activities carried out by the International Physical Protection Advisory Service through

[115] International Atomic Energy Agency (IAEA) Board of Governors: Nuclear Verification and Security Materials (Physical Protection Objectives and Fundamental Principles), IAEA document, GOV/2001/41, 15 Aug. 2001.

[116] Dodd, B., 'The International Atomic Energy Agency's response to the radiological terrorism threat', *Österreichische Militärische Zeitschrift*, special edition, Aug. 2003.

[117] Rauf, T., 'Enhanced physical protection measures and the Agency's plan of action for protection against nuclear terrorism', Presentation at the 2003 NPT PrepCom, Geneva, 6 May 2003. Tariq Rauf is the Head of Verification and Security Policy at the IAEA.

which the IAEA puts together teams of national experts drawn from member states to provide assistance to them on request.

There are clearly important advantages to be gained from helping the IAEA to help its member states find practical means of implementation. The IAEA has itself suggested that it might become a more active player in providing assistance to member states to allow them to implement identified improvements in national systems and to make national systems compliant with the highest agreed standards. The commitments made in the framework of the G8 might provide the IAEA with the funds to play a direct role in project development and implementation, while donor states might see the use of the agency in this way as an efficient and safe way to achieve their CTR objectives. In future, the IAEA may be important as a CTR assistance provider as well as continuing to play a central role in establishing standards and setting objectives for CTR.

The practical disarmament initiative

As noted above, a wider attack on the medium of international air transport—that is, an effort to reduce confidence in air transport rather than attacks on a specific aircraft—has been identified as one possible strategy of mass-impact terrorism. Consequently, there is a need to enhance aviation safety, including by the closer control of conventional weapons that can be used to attack airborne targets. The G8 has, as noted in section III above, made the issue of controls over MANPADS one focus of its attention. In implementing its Action Plan on MANPADS, the G8 might make use of processes that have already been established, including the United Nations practical disarmament initiative.

The concept of 'practical disarmament' was first elaborated by UN Secretary-General Boutros Boutros-Ghali in 1995 in his Agenda for Peace.[118] On 10 December 1996 the General Assembly adopted a resolution on the consolidation of peace through practical disarmament.[119] On 9 December 1997 it established the Group of Interested States (GIS) to oversee the implementation of the initiative.[120] The

---

[118] On the June 1992 Agenda for Peace and the January 1995 Supplement to an Agenda for Peace, see UN document A/47/277 (S/24111) and UN document A/50/60 (S/1995/1), respectively.

[119] UN General Assembly Resolution 51/45N33, 10 Dec. 1996.

[120] UN General Assembly Resolution 52/438G, 9 Dec. 1997.

GIS began its work in 1998 and has gained experience in managing projects combining the efforts of different countries to bring about practical disarmament through the counting, collection and disposal of small arms and light weapons (SALW). These projects share some features of CTR measures.

The idea of practical disarmament was developed for application in a case, SALW, where there were no agreed international measures— although the idea was subsequently incorporated into the UN Programme of Action on Small Arms and Light Weapons in 2001.[121]

Practical disarmament has been characterized as a partnership arrangement. However, projects consist of assistance measures to one state, a developing nation that requests assistance, from one or more other states—developed nations that have both the willingness and the technical and financial capacities to assist.

The United Nations has provided the framework for the GIS to develop their cooperation. The representatives of countries participating in the GIS meet every two or three months in meetings hosted by the German Permanent Mission to the UN in order to examine requests for assistance with practical disarmament, review and evaluate projects being carried out, exchange information about lessons learned from projects and disseminate these lessons. The meetings are also open to participation by non-state representatives that could make a contribution of some kind to achieving the objectives of practical disarmament—for example, the UN Department for Disarmament Affairs and the UN Development Programme (UNDP).

Projects are generated through a process initiated by states that require assistance. These states address their requests for assistance to the interested states, which do not incur any financial or political obligations through their participation in the group. In spite of the informal nature of this arrangement, between 1998 and 2000 over 40 states were involved in the GIS, which had carried out projects in Albania, Cameroon, Guatemala and Niger.

The projects that have been undertaken have been small and have often had the character of pilot projects to test a particular approach or idea. Where the feasibility of a particular project has been demon-

---

[121] United Nations, Programme of Action to Prevent, Combat and Eradicate the Illicit Trade in Small Arms and Light Weapons in All Its Aspects, UN document A/CONF.192/15, 20 July 2001, URL <http://disarmament2.un.org/cab/poa.html> .

strated, this has, in some cases, led to larger projects organized outside the framework of the GIS and sponsored by, for example, the UNDP.

The North Atlantic Treaty Organization

NATO is an organization that has the potential to define and implement CTR projects as well as some experience in project management.

During the 1990s a number of statements made under the auspices of NATO demonstrated a growing appreciation that shared concerns related to NBC weapons should be addressed within the NATO framework. At the 1999 Washington Summit the Heads of State and Government approved a new strategic doctrine that committed NATO to 'actively contribute' to the development of arms control, disarmament and non-proliferation agreements as well as to enhance political efforts to reduce the dangers arising from the proliferation of WMD and their means of delivery.[122]

NATO has established a Senior Politico-Military Group on Proliferation (SGP) to address the political dimensions of its response to proliferation, including discussion of the political and economic means to prevent it.[123]

In May 2000 the NATO Weapons of Mass Destruction Centre was opened to provide a focal point for NATO expertise and to support the work of the SGP.[124] The centre comprises an interdisciplinary team with expertise in CW, biological agents, ballistic missiles, force protection, intelligence, and political aspects of arms control and non-proliferation regimes. The broad objectives of the WMD Centre include strengthening the exchange of information concerning national programmes for bilateral WMD destruction and assistance, with a particular emphasis on Russia.

[122] NATO, The Alliance's Strategic Concept approved by the Heads of State and Government participating in the meeting of the North Atlantic Council in Washington, DC, on 23–24 Apr. 1999, press release NAC-S(99)65, 24 Apr. 1999, URL <http://www.nato.int/docu/pr/1999/p99-065e.htm>.

[123] See NATO Handbook, Chapter 13: key to the principal NATO committees and to institutions of cooperation, partnership and dialogue, Key to the principal NATO committees, Senior Politico-Military Group on Proliferation, URL <http://www.nato.int/docu/handbook/2001/hb130116.htm>.

[124] NATO, On-line library fact sheet, Weapons of Mass Destruction Centre, URL <http://www.nato.int/docu/facts/2000/wmd.htm>.

In this context it should also be mentioned that the WMD Centre helps support the work of the NATO Senior Political Committee,[125] which prepares the activities of the NATO–Russia Council.[126] The Council was established in 2002 to provide a forum in which NATO member states and Russia could work as equal partners in areas of common interest. Among the areas defined was non-proliferation, including exploring opportunities for intensified practical cooperation.

As part of the process of deeper cooperation between NATO and Russia an Information, Consultation and Training Centre was established in Moscow in June 2001 to support a programme intended to help individuals from the Russian armed forces prepare for demobilization.[127] The Moscow centre, which began its operations in March 2002, will train individuals who will, in turn, run courses in different parts of Russia to help former servicemen make a successful transition to civilian life. This project, while small, is intended to lead to the development of other forms of cooperation on human resource issues.

In addition to the development of bilateral cooperation with Russia, NATO has carried out operational activities in the framework of its Partnership for Peace (PFP) programme through which experience is being gained that might be applicable to CTR.

After 1999 NATO made its expertise in demilitarization and recycling available to states that participate in the PFP, and has assisted in a number of specific projects. Countries that are interested in receiving assistance with demilitarization may apply to the Political–Military Steering Committee (PMSC) on the PFP, the basic working body with responsibility for PFP matters.[128]

A proposal from a partner country must always include a NATO member as a sponsor and a NATO member as a designated lead nation—although the inclusion of non-NATO countries such as Switzerland as lead nations is currently under consideration. However, any state or organization may contribute to a project. The

---

[125] NATO Handbook (note 123), Senior Political Committee, URL <http://www.nato.int/docu/handbook/2001/hb130112.htm>.

[126] NATO, Russian relations: a new quality, 6 Jan 2004, URL <http://www.nato.int/issues/nato-russia/nato-russia.htm>.

[127] NATO, 'Opening of an information, consultation and training centre in Moscow', 20 Mar. 2002, URL <http://www.nato.int/docu/update/2002/03-march/e0320c.htm>.

[128] See NATO Handbook, Chapter 3: the opening up of the alliance, Partnership for Peace, Political–Military Steering Committee on Partnership for Peace, URL <http://www.nato.int/docu/handbook/2001/hb030205.htm>.

PMSC acts as a clearing house to spread information about prospective and current projects. Through the PMSC countries may find other partners interested and able to contribute to some aspect of project implementation.

As an information clearing house, the PFP approach performs a similar role to that of the GIS within the UN—albeit with a more limited geographical emphasis. However, the PFP is supported by other agencies that can play a more direct role in helping to manage and implement projects.

The project applicants are able to receive assistance from the International Staff of NATO in the Defence Planning and Operations Division when preparing the project application. Moreover, if a project is approved it may be implemented and financed under NATO auspices.

The NATO Maintenance and Supply Agency (NAMSA) is NATO's principal logistics support management agency.[129] Its main purpose is to oversee projects providing 'cradle to grave' logistical services to support about 30 designated weapon system types. Its services are invoked when two or more NATO member states decide that contracting with NAMSA is more cost-effective than supporting their equipment independently using national means. Through these activities NAMSA has gained significant project management expertise in a range of tasks including demilitarization and the recycling of weapons and ammunition. NAMSA has developed an alliance-wide contact network of technical experts because it has worked with contractors to demilitarize most types of land, sea and air munitions, including mines, cluster bombs, rockets and guided missiles, as well as many types of high explosives and pyrotechnics.

Using NAMSA to manage projects for demilitarization increases confidence in the selection of contractors, in the writing of contracts and project specifications, and in monitoring contract performance through to completion. NAMSA is obliged to evaluate the environmental impact of demilitarization processes and ensure that they conform with accepted standards. NAMSA contracts with a commercial firm to demilitarize the equipment and it is the commercial contractor that receives equipment scheduled for demilitarization. Depending on the wishes of the customer, either the contractor can carry out the full

---

[129] See NATO Handbook, Chapter 14: key to organizations and agencies and other subordinate bodies, logistics, NATO Maintenance and Supply Agency, URL <http://www.nato.int/docu/handbook/2001/hb140203.htm>.

range of demilitarization tasks or, should it be necessary, some of these tasks can be undertaken by military personnel. The PFP Trust Fund can finance certain types of project.[130] The fund is replenished on a project basis. Any nation interested in a particular project, whether a member of NATO or not, can contribute to the fund in the knowledge that the contribution will be used only for that particular project. Projects carried out by NAMSA have also on occasion generated revenue through their recycling activities.[131] Initially, only one type of project (the destruction of anti-personnel landmines) was eligible for financing through the PFP Trust Fund. However, in 2001 the scope of the fund was widened to include other types of demilitarization projects.

By mid-2003 NAMSA was engaged in or had completed demilitarization projects funded by NATO's PFP Trust Fund in Albania, Azerbaijan, Belarus, Georgia, Moldova, Serbia and Montenegro, Ukraine and Uzbekistan. Moreover, the scope of projects has expanded from a limited focus on landmines to include demilitarization projects to dispose of missiles, rocket fuel, and small arms and ammunition.

NATO members have also recognized that the scope of work undertaken in this field of demilitarization should be widened further. The extension of the role of the PMSC clearing house to facilitate bilateral assistance is envisaged in the decisions taken at the 2002 Prague NATO Summit.[132] The development of cooperation with the EU, the Organization for Security and Co-operation in Europe and NGOs is also envisaged.

VI. Conclusions

This chapter demonstrates that a variety of mechanisms and processes are being used to establish objectives for and coordinate the activities of CTR programmes. While these programmes all underline the need to avoid duplication in coordination efforts, there are nevertheless

---

[130] The PFP Trust Fund was first established as part of the NATO contribution to implementing its programme on Global Humanitarian Mine Action.

[131] E.g., the Coca Cola Company has purchased white phosphorus reclaimed from weapon demilitarization.

[132] NATO, 'Report on the comprehensive review of the Euro-Atlantic Partnership Council and Partnership for Peace', press release, Prague Summit, 21 Nov. 2002, URL <http://www.nato.int/docu/basictxt/b021121a.htm>.

certain overlaps. At the same time, these processes all add to the wider CTR in different ways.

No standard technique is ever likely to be applicable in all cases. There is, therefore, no attempt made here to suggest that one form of organization is superior to the others or should automatically be the first preference. Nevertheless, in thinking about which would be the appropriate procedures to apply in any given case it might be useful to identify the advantages and disadvantages of the various approaches.

The EU has the widest spectrum of capacities within the framework. It is able to establish policies, both for its member states and for the common institutions, to mobilize the resources needed to develop and implement projects and to supervise implementation. The EU is making a concerted effort to develop a security strategy and a strategy against the proliferation of WMD. The further development of CTR measures will play a part in this wider effort. While the EU has relations with most countries of the world, in the first instance the primary area of application for new measures is likely to be Europe, particularly around the periphery of the enlarged EU.

Prior to the recent decisions of the EU, these issues were only discussed at expert level in the European institutions and among a handful of individuals. While the issues are now higher on the political agenda, it remains the case that the total number of people within the EU who are responsible for implementing the decisions taken is small and they are scattered across different parts of the Council and the European Commission.

The G8 participating states are particularly active in trying to promote the idea of CTR as a security-building measure. During 2002 and 2003 the G8 established that it could mobilize significant high-level political support behind CTR initiatives. The Senior Officials Group, established to assist in implementing the Global Partnership, could point to some significant achievements and innovations during its first year. The extent to which the G8 can sustain this political support is not possible to determine at present. However, given the past record of the G8 and its lack of institutional resources there is a doubt about whether any programme could be sustained over a 10-year period under its auspices alone. The extent to which the G8 makes an impact over the longer term depends on the extent to which the issues around CTR become part of the agenda in more permanent institutions.

Over time the Moscow-based ISTC has evolved from organizing external technical assistance into a more genuinely international centre. The decision to establish ISTC offices in other countries of the FSU indicates that states are willing to consider reproducing the ISTC-type approach in other countries.[133] However, it has not been possible to evaluate how far the ISTC has been able to achieve its primary objective of facilitating the transfer of human resources out of the NBC weapon development and production complex.

To date, the UN has not generally been considered to have played a central role in CTR. However, the IAEA is in the process of developing a broad and ambitious programme to reduce the risk of nuclear terrorism. In addition, the IAEA is increasingly taking security-related issues into account when conducting many of its activities. The UN has also demonstrated that it can help states to organize and implement some practical disarmament measures that could play a role in identifying, securing, reducing and eliminating weapon stockpiles that currently lack adequate controls.

Similarly, NATO has been thought not to have a significant role to play in CTR. However, it possesses all of the elements that would be required to play a more important role and has shown some indications that it might be inclined to develop and use these assets in a coherent fashion. NATO has begun to develop a policy framework for addressing WMD, an institutional framework for interacting with Russia, and it often uses NAMSA for demilitarization projects. The idea of using a designated lead nation to take responsibility for coordinating contributions by several donors in the framework of a bilateral project is also a potentially valuable innovation in terms of project organization. A 'country sectorization', in which specific countries are given the job of coordinating activities in specific areas, could be envisaged in future as the number of CTR projects grows. For example, Norway is already developing a specialization in dismantling nuclear submarines. France might choose to concentrate on nuclear fissile material and Germany on CW destruction.

Individual countries are also beginning to offer project management services to other donors that want to contribute to CTR but which

---

[133] E.g., the Science and Technology Center in Ukraine (STCU) was established in Kyiv in 1993, more or less in parallel with the International Science and Technology Center. See the STCU Internet site at URL <http://www.stcu.int>.

might have been deterred had they been required to establish a separate national programme.[134] Taken together, these coordination processes are sufficient basis for the expansion and strengthening of CTR that is currently required. Within the framework of these processes, states should be able to identify the items of greatest current concern and mobilize the technical and financial resources that would enable projects to come to fruition

---

[134] E.g., Canada is exploring whether to make a contribution to CW destruction by providing support under the auspices of a project led by the UK.

3. Cooperative threat reduction project management and implementation

I. Introduction

Chapter 2 described the development of the coordination mechanisms that attempt to identify, facilitate and finance CTR projects. However, the participants in these coordination mechanisms have stressed that they are not responsible for implementing projects. Projects have often been developed to assist in the implementation of agreements or to help states implement political commitments that they have undertaken. The providers of assistance have stressed that CTR does not reduce the responsibility of states to meet their commitments and obligations, and therefore responsibility for project implementation must rest primarily with the authorities of the country in which the project is being carried out.

While the G8 in particular has tried to adopt a proactive position to encourage more CTR projects, project initiatives come from countries that require assistance. Within the G8 other members consider project proposals brought to them by Russia and do not propose new projects to Russia. While the G8 Senior Officials Group already conducts some outreach activities, the G8 countries require an approach from governments seeking to join the Global Partnership before any projects can be defined.

Many of the questions that surround project definition—including project objectives, actors and partners, costs, and timescales—should already have been addressed before external donors are approached. Because CTR has been characterized by 'learning by doing', in reality, the process of project definition almost certainly needs to be iterative because few of these questions are likely to have been answered definitively at the outset of project discussions. As more experience is gained with CTR, countries seeking assistance should be able to improve their capacity to develop a comprehensive project proposal. Similarly, countries prepared to offer assistance need to be able to evaluate the proposals they receive.

A significant amount of information about past experiences with CTR project implementation is available from studies of projects carried out in Russia and Ukraine, in cooperation with the USA in particular. A more limited amount of information is available from projects carried out in other countries. This information also largely reflects the US experience in countries that have emerged on the territory of the FSU.

The fact that most project descriptions are of US–Russian efforts is problematic in that the bilateral projects between these countries have probably tended to be larger and more complex than those undertaken in Russia by other countries or in countries other than Russia. However, certain common characteristics of project management and implementation are apparent from existing case studies.

Any project will have to address certain generic issues, including: project definition, establishing a legal basis for projects, costing and financing, contractor selection, oversight (including project evaluation and reporting), and audit.

The customer for CTR projects is almost certain to be a government or state agency. Where projects focus on weapon stockpile security, consolidation, monitoring or destruction this customer is likely to be a ministry (probably a defence ministry but possibly also an interior ministry) or a branch of the armed forces. Where projects focus on other kinds of activity, the customer might be a different branch of the central state apparatus—such as the ministry responsible for atomic energy or an economic ministry.

Threat reduction projects have often generated subsidiary activities with other types of customer, such as agencies of regional and local government or local suppliers of equipment and services. To illustrate, in 1992 President Yeltsin announced the decision to construct a pilot facility at Gorny to test and validate technology for the destruction of CW in the most environmentally safe manner. Destruction operations at Gorny began in December 2002.[135] Russia developed the scientific and technical methodology used in destruction and constructed the destruction facility. However, during the course of this process Russia received significant foreign assistance from a number of countries.

Germany was the main source of external assistance and provided a large amount of heavy, specialized equipment for the plant. Finland developed and installed equipment to detect chemical leakages from the plant and trained local personnel to operate and maintain the equipment. The EU TACIS programme financed the development of a

---

[135] Hart, J., Kuhlau, F. and Simon, J., 'Chemical and biological weapon developments and arms control', *SIPRI Yearbook 2003* (note 19), p. 656.

wider environmental monitoring system around Gorny. This system has played an important role in reassuring the local population about the safety of the destruction operation, which has in turn reduced local opposition to the decision to locate the plant in Gorny. The Netherlands has provided equipment to help establish a reliable supply of electricity to the plant. During the period of developing and testing technical approaches to destruction, specialists from the UK and the Organisation for the Prohibition of Chemical Weapons have provided training to Russian Munitions Agency personnel and other Russian scientists and officials.[136] In talks with potential assistance donors Russia has raised the question of how to support the cost of providing amenities (housing, communications, water and electricity) for the military and civilian personnel that will operate the plant. However, donors have not been willing to provide this assistance and the costs have fallen to Russia.

This demonstrates that a project to construct a CW destruction plant has actually generated a number of activities (some of which were unanticipated when the original project was conceived) that have been treated separately from a contractual and financial perspective. However, carrying out these activities has been critical to the overall success of the programme.

A number of different contractual arrangements are possible. A local supplier could be contracted by the customer to provide the necessary equipment and services. Alternatively, the customer might contract with a foreign prime contractor. A third alternative, a 'twinning' arrangement, could pair domestic and foreign contractors to perform particular tasks either through the formation of a joint venture or through the creation of an international project team.

While there has been a growing tendency to stress partnership as the basis for CTR, the fact that a foreign donor is financing all or part of the project is a factor that has to be taken into account in project design. Where the customer and the supplier are both located in the project country the external contributions might be financial and/or the provision of specialist equipment or services.

---

[136] Deffrennes, M., 'Programmes in the field of non-proliferation and disarmament', Unpublished paper, Dec. 2002. Marc Deffrennes is Head of Sector, WMD non-proliferation and disarmament, at the European Commission.

The project design must include features which satisfy the assistance provider that the project will be carried out and that resources will be used in a responsible and honest manner. This need not entail intrusive monitoring or verification of a type that has sometimes been used in arms control agreements. A systematic gathering of information, regular reporting and opportunities for discussion and clarification must be designed to meet the national accountability requirements of the donor and to ensure compliance with the donor's national export control regulations. As suggested above, this might involve different reporting requirements in cases where there are multiple assistance donors. The contract arrangements need to make provisions for the disclosure of the information needed to satisfy these requirements.

In cases where the customer selects a company from the assistance donor country to act as a prime contractor or to provide equipment and/or services directly, there is a need to ensure that the arrangements permit physical access for representatives of the foreign contractor as well as the disclosure of information that the contractor needs to complete the agreed tasks. However, in this case the assistance donor may make payments directly to the prime contractor, which is located in its own country. Contracts therefore need to provide the customer with information about the way in which the contractor carries out the project and a means of redress in case a project is not implemented in a satisfactory manner. Authorities of the assistance donor will still need to be satisfied with reporting mechanisms and information provision in order to ensure accountability.

From these brief observations it is clear that effective implementation will depend heavily on the steps taken by the customer in the country where projects are being carried out. Many of the implementation difficulties that have hampered past projects reflect the lack of a comprehensive, consistent and transparent approach in the project country.

II. The emerging preference for a partnership approach

An expansion of the geographical scope of CTR is anticipated in future. However, in the short term most projects will be implemented in Russia. This is partly because of the scale of the residual tasks in Russia and partly because there are a large number of mature projects close to being ready for implementation. While Russia's experience is certainly unique, there are aspects of project implementation in Russia that might yield general lessons of value to other countries.

The Russian experience suggests that the implementation of CTR projects can be seriously hampered if a number of 'top–down' issues are not addressed in the country where the projects are being carried out. Only the authorities in that country can determine the place of CTR in overall national policy. Only sustained engagement by officials at a high level can produce cooperation between different national ministries and authorities whose participation and assent is required for project implementation.[137]

In Russia experience suggests that regional authorities do not identify CTR measures as a high priority. Projects are judged against the contribution that activities make to the local economy and environment and not against national security considerations.[138]

The specific conditions in Russia in the 1990s made it very difficult to establish an overall policy towards CTR and to clarify its place within wider national policy. However, practical experience has demonstrated that a strategic 'master plan' is needed to allow external contributions to be fully utilized and sustained.

Whether or not this overall plan should be embedded into national legislation and whether particular dedicated institutions are needed to implement it remain open questions in Russia. At present there is no specific legislation establishing binding rules for the different elements of CTR. Nevertheless, the personal engagement of President Vladimir Putin in the framework of the G8 Global Partnership has allowed progress to be made on a number of issues that had previously been deadlocked. For example, domestic implementing measures needed to provide indemnity from certain kinds of liability for contractors as well as tax and other exemptions for project-related assistance are to be managed through the issue of presidential waivers

---

[137] Moreover, a national authority is able to promote information exchange and, where needed, facilitate coordination between different regional authorities.

[138] The mayor of Kambarka was quoted as saying that only after a local sewage system, water supply and natural gas supply as well as a new hospital and an upgraded road network had been provided should the plant to destroy chemical weapons be constructed. Similar comments have been attributed to his counterpart in the town of Schuchye. Bobrov, V., 'Ischadie ada' [The thing from hell], *Profile*, 19 May 1997; and Litovkin, V., 'Fruktovy zapah otravy' [The fruit flavour of poison], *Ogonek*, 2 Oct. 1995.

to current Russian legislation rather than through legislative amendments.

In Russia, since the establishment of the Global Partnership, an intergovernmental group of officials has met monthly to evaluate and authorize CTR activities without the need for further consultations. These officials are drawn from specialized units that have been established within all relevant ministries and can, if necessary, count on the high-level engagement of the Presidential Administration. This arrangement should accelerate project implementation and might also help to simplify the procedures for obtaining approval for different project activities. In the past the need to receive approval from many different ministries, agencies and authorities before a particular activity could be carried out has been mentioned as one reason for project delays.[139]

The political conditions are currently favourable to CTR projects in Russia because of the degree of engagement by the president and because of the changed nature of Russian relations with the USA and the West in general. However, the CTR programme already defined with Russia will require projects to be implemented over a period of more than 10 years and, given the past record, it may not be a safe assumption that this extended period will always be characterized by a positive spirit in relations with Russia.

There may be an opportunity at present to establish an enduring and binding legal and administrative framework for CTR. Russian domestic legislation could replace the current need to negotiate separate agreements on a sectoral or project basis and would ensure that external contributors to projects were treated in an even-handed manner. Some Russian analysts have argued in favour of such a legal framework.[140] However, holding discussions with the Russian Parliament on, for example, making exemptions to Russian tax law that would apply to all CTR projects carries the risk that parliamentarians would use the opportunity to attempt a broad legislative review of the Russian tax system and that this review would introduce delays. These delays might represent a lost opportunity to develop project activities in the current positive climate.

---

[139] Remarks by Natalya Kalinina (note 108). The steps taken by President Putin to increase the degree of federal oversight and control of regional authorities in Russia are also important background factors that could help to simplify the process of project implementation.

[140] Kalinina (note 16).

While, hypothetically, domestic legislation might help to insulate the implementation of CTR projects from future political changes, at present there are no plans to introduce such legislation. The main priority in Russia appears to be to use the current opportunity to make progress on project implementation and thereby perhaps develop greater domestic support for and more momentum behind CTR.

The Russian experience suggests that an overall plan should include codifying an agreed set of priorities to facilitate project evaluation and resource allocation decisions. The decision about which projects to carry out and in what sequence should be heavily influenced by the priorities of the country where projects are proposed vis-à-vis weapon non-proliferation, environmental concerns, disarmament obligations, counter-terrorism, and perhaps also social and humanitarian considerations where these are a barrier to security building. These national priorities, if codified in an agreed document after widespread consultation, would help partners to make their decisions about project support, for example, to decide whether to support projects that emphasize the containment of a problem (through physical protection and safe storage) over a more permanent solution (through destruction and liquidation).

The preparation of a national plan can also facilitate domestic transparency in CTR, which has proved to be a difficult issue in Russia, where many participants have been dissatisfied with the quality of either the inter-agency consultation process or the information provided to parliament and the public.

While the level of Russian national contributions to CTR projects has increased in recent years, there is not sufficient transparency on the Russian side to judge whether budget decisions have actually led to an increase in resources. Russian observers have pointed out that, in spite of the increased value of the budget lines for CTR projects, not much money actually seems to have been spent.

The existence of a national plan would also reduce the risk that CTR will be seen as an imposition from abroad. Since the 1990s there has been a progressive move away from seeing CTR as technical assistance, with donor countries setting priorities and project objectives, and towards a partnership approach in which all parties feel common 'ownership' and therefore a strong commitment to the overall programme.

The role of institutions that will be both directly affected by and engaged in implementing CTR in the process of defining an overall approach needs to be given careful consideration. The exclusion of the military and defence establishment, the nuclear establishment or other powerful institutions from the process of defining a national programme might subsequently lead these bodies to obstruct implementation of an approach that they do not support or that they feel does not provide them with fair representation. These institutions need to be persuaded that they have a stake and a self-interest in the implementation of CTR projects.

Similarly, political institutions other than the executive branch need to understand the role of CTR in national policy and to be convinced of its merits. This includes representatives in the national parliament as well as local government, including both the local executive branch and local representatives.

Taking the case of Russia, for a number of years important individuals within the relevant bureaucracies and in the national parliament remained unconvinced that implementation of CTR was in the national interest. Prior to the inclusion of Russia in the G8 and the creation of the Global Partnership a lot of time was lost in overcoming the suspicion that CTR was a cover for espionage or part of an external drive to take advantage of a weak Russia and prevent the recovery of its military and economic capacities.[141] This domestic obstructionism has been identified even when the projects were intended to help Russia meet its obligations under international agreements such as the START I Treaty and the CWC. While traces of this attitude still remain in Russia where the USA is concerned, assistance from European countries or from the EU is not usually seen from this perspective.

A national plan could help to identify, marginalize or even remove key officials who are not committed to the implementation of agreed goals. However, it cannot solve deeper problems. For example, it has not been possible to implement comprehensive projects on BW-related issues because of the difficulty of finding a customer on the Russian side interested in contracting for such projects. This reflects the absence of an agreed position and different degrees of concern

---

[141] In the initial phases of the CTR programme even US assistance with the effort to consolidate nuclear weapons in secure locations was described in the Russian Federation's Congress of People's Deputies, by some Russian parliamentarians, as an act of national betrayal.

between Russia and CTR project partners about Russian BW-related activities. The development of a national plan could help to clarify and set aside areas that are not promising for CTR initiatives.

The need for a national plan based on widespread consultation could have an impact on the thinking of assistance donor countries about the anticipated life span of CTR programmes. In essence, it should be assumed from the outset that both an overall country programme and specific projects will involve sustained multi-year engagement and therefore require a financial and administrative framework able to accommodate and support activities through cycles much longer than 12 months.

Outreach activities should stress the need for countries that may need CTR assistance to develop a country strategy document to assist in project definition and to help prepare a detailed request for assistance. While it is not possible to propose a rigid time frame, planners should probably use a five-year cycle as the basis for their initial planning and also prepare for project continuation into a follow-up period of around five years.

If the main future priority for CTR is counter-terrorism, and in order to target terrorist-related CTR outreach activities, it would be necessary to organize consultations on which countries most need assistance in this sphere and, at the same time, to establish a list of which countries are considered to meet the Kananaskis criteria.

Not all issues and questions need to be considered by a national body and the preparation of a national plan should not be incompatible with a 'bottom–up' approach where Russian technical expertise and knowledge is actively included in the process of project definition from the very beginning. On the contrary, the clarity provided by a national plan should help to create confidence that project implementation is taking place within agreed guidelines and can therefore be left to the responsible parties.

It is possible to argue that Russian experts know how to solve many of the technical problems that arise during projects and that it may also be easier for them to resolve, for example, access issues by dealing with them on a practical basis at a working level rather than on a political basis in high-level talks. Russian entities and managers are more likely to understand the legislative requirements and the bureaucratic process that will need to be navigated during the establishment and implementation of a project. Through a bottom–up approach many problems that made cooperation more difficult may be circumvented with little fanfare.

Case studies have suggested that one of the most serious barriers to project implementation has been the fact that Russian central authorities, ministries and agencies have not been psychologically prepared to accept a bottom–up approach that they feel gives them too little insight into and control over projects.

Progamme management in Ukraine

The approach to programme management followed by Ukraine is different from that followed by Russia.[142] In Ukraine the Centre to Support the Implementation of Agreements was established within the Ukrainian Ministry of Defence to take responsibility for project management under the general oversight and guidance of the National Security and Defence Council (NSDC) of Ukraine. The centre cooperates closely with its counterpart in the US Department of Defense. The NSDC, which reports directly to Ukraine's Presidential Administration, has an ad hoc Interdepartmental Working Group, led by the Deputy Minister of Defence, that prepares materials for meetings of the council. The working group includes high-level representatives from ministries and agencies and representatives from industries that deal with CTR issues.[143] This structure was created to provide all of the agencies associated with different tasks with information and a voice in decision making.

A US prime contractor, chosen by the US Government, selects subcontractors among Ukrainian companies to carry out practical implementation tasks associated with US assistance. The prime contractor

[142] Chumak, V., Research Centre for Nonproliferation Problems (Kyiv), *Cooperative Threat Reduction in Ukraine*, Paper presented to the Nonproliferation and Export Control Working Group, Partnership for Peace Consortium of Defence Academies, Paris, July 2002.

[143] E.g., in the project to eliminate SS-24 ballistic missiles in Ukraine the Ministry of Defence is responsible for the safe custody of missiles prior to elimination; the Ministry of Industrial Policy is responsible for overseeing the dismantlement and elimination of the missiles, processing materials and waste, implementing conversion programmes and related activities; the Ministry of Transport is responsible for the safe transport of missiles by rail; the Ministry of Ecology and Natural Resources monitors compliance with ecological regulations; the Ministry of Foreign Affairs is responsible for ensuring consistency between international and domestic legal regulations; and the Aviation and Space Agency participates in the conversion of the space and missile industry as well as extracting and reprocessing SS-24 solid missile fuel (carried out together with the Pavlograd Chemical Plant).

receives money from the US Government and, in turn, makes payments to Ukrainian contractors and cooperates with the Ukrainian authorities to ensure delivery of equipment and machinery.

Management through a designated prime contractor has proved to be an effective way to provide funds while making sure that the programme complies with US reporting requirements. The need to conform to the cash management practices of the US contractor reduces the risk of theft or diversion of funds for purposes that are irrelevant to the programme. Moreover, working with the US contractor has the additional indirect benefit of providing Ukrainian entities with experience of international project management.

III. Contractor selection and allocating project responsibilities

Once a project has been defined it is necessary to select the various project members and define their responsibilities.

As noted above, the customer for a project is the government or state authority of the country in which the project is being implemented. However, a framework agreement between governments is not specific enough to meet the donors' need for accountability in the use of resources provided. The contract needs to specify more precisely who is responsible for carrying out necessary tasks, the timetable for work, and the degree of information and oversight allowed to the various parties.

Contractor selection in Ukraine

In Ukraine, private companies from the USA have implemented CTR projects in whole or in part under contract to a specially created agency within the Ukrainian Ministry of Defence. The US prime contractor has, in turn, subcontracted with Ukrainian enterprises to carry out many elements of the project. This arrangement requires the US prime contractor rather than the Ukrainian Ministry of Defence to pay Ukrainian subcontractors for the services that they provide. In these conditions, the financial transfer from the donor country to the country where the project is being implemented is greater. The subcontracting arrangement requires an agreed costing of equipment and services provided locally, a difficult issue that is discussed further in section IV below.

The use of a foreign prime contractor requires the creation of a legal framework that guarantees physical access to locations where project work is taking place. In Ukraine this was not a particularly contentious issue because of the nature of the projects—the destruction of strategic delivery systems, launch facilities and associated infrastructure that Ukraine had already decided it no longer wished to retain and that were subject to the terms of the START I Treaty. These background conditions are very different from those prevailing in Russia, where sensitivities about controlled access for non-Russian project staff or staff lacking required clearances have been much greater.

In an indication of the degree to which this is still a live issue in spite of recent cooperation, a joint US Congress and Norwegian Ministry of Foreign Affairs delegation to the Nerpa shipyard in Russia was denied access to the site at which both countries are preparing to finance nuclear submarine decommissioning. The Russian Ministry of Defence apparently objected to the presence of six members of the US–Norwegian delegation.[144] This is only one example among many of the access difficulties that have occurred in CTR projects.

Contractor selection in Russia

In Russia, the customers for CTR projects had little experience with either writing or enforcing contracts of the kind required by the governments providing external assistance. Moreover, the providers of assistance to Russia have been put in the unfamiliar position of having to work within their own rules for contracting and cash management without having the degree of control over projects that they would normally have.

Of the 43 project agreements that Russia has signed with other states and organizations, most (25) have been signed by the Ministry of Atomic Energy.[145] The Russian Munitions Agency has been the

[144] Digges, C., 'Members of US–Norwegian delegation barred from dismantlement shipyard', Bellona, 13 Aug. 2003, URL <http://www.bellona.no/en/international/russia/nuke_industry/co-operation/30690.html>.

[145] Einhorn, R. and Flournoy, M. (eds), Center for Strategic and International Studies (CSIS), *Protecting Against the Spread of Nuclear, Biological and Chemical Weapons: An action agenda for the Global Partnership*, vol. 4, *Russian Perspectives and Priorities* (CSIS Press: Washington, DC, 2003), p. 8.

main customer for seven projects and the Ministry of Defence for six. Other designated customers have included the Ministry of Economic Development and Trade, the Russian Aviation and Space Agency, and the Federal Nuclear and Radiation Safety Authority.

These customers have, in turn, had to coordinate with other federal entities and regional authorities. For example, of the 25 projects for which MINATOM was the main customer, 8 required supplementary inter-agency agreements. In addition to the supplementary agreements laying out the respective rights and obligations of different parties in the country where the project is being carried out, an inter-agency mechanism is required for monitoring the performance of agreed tasks and for information sharing as well as to resolve any disputes or obstacles to implementation. Experience has suggested that this inter-agency group should be made up of high-level representatives of their respective ministries or agencies.

Under CTR project arrangements there is a question that does not normally arise in market transactions—the degree to which the main customer for a project may set the terms and conditions for contractors.

The customer has limited choice of contractors in many of the projects undertaken because there may only be one, or a handful, of specialized agencies or enterprises with the competence to perform the necessary tasks. In these conditions a project is being implemented through a more or less closed arrangement between state-owned authorities that know each other well and have a long history of cooperation. This model does not require a major transfer of funds to the country where the project is being carried out. The implementing agencies use equipment and/or technology provided by the external donor. This requires a subcontracting arrangement between the domestic agency or enterprise responsible for project implementation and foreign suppliers to ensure site access for the delivery and installation of equipment, to provide training in its use, and to perform repairs and maintenance. However, the payments for equipment and services would be made to the foreign supplier by the donor government.

It may be the case that the agency responsible for project implementation finds itself implementing a project about which it has misgivings. In the worst case scenario, under the contracting arrangement outlined above, both the customer and project managers may resent having to contribute some of their own scarce resources to implement a project that they had little role in designing and that they believe to be contrary to their institutional interests or perhaps even contrary to the national interest. Purely domestic contracting arrangements will make it very difficult for external agencies to have much oversight or direct influence over the conduct of project activities.

In some cases there have been attempts to mitigate these potentially negative situations through the creation of additional incentives. For example, US-sponsored nuclear safety projects with MINATOM have included provisions that any technologies and processes developed will be owned by the agency. These, as well as being applied in Russia, can subsequently be used in commercial activities—such as the sale of nuclear safety services to other countries operating Soviet-designed installations.[146]

Such potential problems underscore the value of a comprehensive national plan developed by the project country that anchors projects in national policy and requires regular and transparent reporting.

While the experience gained in project implementation in both Russia and Ukraine suggests that whenever possible local expertise should be used during CTR activities, there have been different approaches to project management in the two countries.

The twinning of contractors in a partnership is a model that has been followed in, for example, the laboratory-to-laboratory cooperation arrangements between Russia and the USA. These arrangements are intended to lead to the joint development of technologies that can be used in CTR, including enhancing physical security and containment of facilities; fissile material accounting; plutonium disposition; plutonium storage at the Mayak facility in Russia; and monitoring nuclear warhead dismantlement. These activities were carried out under contracts awarded to individual laboratories by the US Department of Energy and the Russian MINATOM. Under these arrangements, joint project teams were able to carry out reciprocal visits as well as share insights and ideas on technical solutions to the problems under review.

---

[146] Jordan, M., Presentation to the Conference on Building Industrial Partnerships in the former Soviet Union, Fort Lesley J. McNair, Washington, DC, 19 Apr. 1995. Michael Jordan is Chairman and Chief Executive of Westinghouse Electric Corporation

This form of twinning within the framework of a specific project allows each of the partners to take the lead in dealing with the reporting and regulatory requirements in respect of their own governments. At the same time the creation of an international project team drawing personnel from both partners allows the partners to apply their collective expertise to the project. Moreover, because within this type of arrangement project teams are likely to have to make a detailed joint appraisal of problems and issues as they arise, an environment should be created in which both sides can learn and improve their performance.

This approach is thought to have led to successful results partly because it was developed 'away from the political spotlight and engaged technical experts who shared both knowledge and appreciation of the issues at a technical level'.[147] However, this pattern of development has also caused delays to the programme because of concerns about how such international project teams can conduct their activities without undermining national requirements to safeguard classified information and national controls on intangible technology transfers.[148]

A fourth form of project organization is also worth mentioning. In many cases small projects that are time-limited can be organized using a simple legal and administrative format. Projects that can be planned and executed within a short time frame (e.g., one year) and that focus on the provision of training may be carried out by a designated entity from the country that provides financial assistance. This entity can take responsibility for the organization of meetings and seminars with an identified partner in the project country and make use of existing arrangements with its domestic authorities to ensure appropriate oversight of implementation and use of resources.

To summarize, under any model the questions surrounding contractor selection, the terms of their contracts and the oversight of their work have all been contentious at times. If the contractor comes from the country that is financing the project and not from the country where the project is carried out, it may face problems in gaining access to locations where it needs to work and in gaining information

---

[147] The programmes for laboratory-to-laboratory cooperation are described in Hafmeister, D., 'US nuclear security cooperation with Russia and transparency', ed. Zarimpas (note 25).

[148] For a discussion on intangible transfers, see Anthony, I., 'Multilateral weapon and technology export controls', *SIPRI Yearbook 2001* (note 81), pp. 631–35.

because its personnel lack the necessary clearances. Conversely, if the contractor comes from the country where the project is being carried out, this can create some additional difficulties in gaining approval for any technology transfer that may be needed to carry out the project.

On balance, however, the greatest possible use of local contractors seems to be the best arrangement, provided that all parties have sufficient trust that projects will be carried out in good faith. However, the building of trust between project partners requires continuity in personnel over an extended period.

Certain problems appear to cut across countries and project types, including the issues of contractor liability and exemption from certain taxes and fees. As noted in chapter 2, projects involve working with equipment and materials that are inherently dangerous and in locations where the terrain and climate are harsh. Assistance donors will probably insist on a legal framework that makes clear who will be legally and financially responsible for taking preventive measures to reduce risks and remedial measures in case of accidents involving services or equipment provided by external companies or agents. The Protocol on Claims, Legal Proceedings and Indemnification[149] to the Framework Agreement on a Multilateral Nuclear Environmental Programme in Russia goes some way to clarifying the issue of liability.

The Protocol establishes rules for cases where project activities cause nuclear damage, which is defined in the document. According to the Protocol

Russian authorities shall bring no claims or legal proceedings of any kind against the contributors and their personnel or contractors, subcontractors, consultants, suppliers or sub-suppliers of equipment, goods or services at any tier and their personnel, for any loss or damage of whatsoever nature, including but not limited to personal injury, loss of life, direct, indirect and consequential damage to property owned by the Russian Federation arising from activities undertaken pursuant to the Agreement.

However, Russian authorities may bring actions if the nuclear damage was caused intentionally and this indemnity does not apply to the enforcement of the provisions written into any specific contract.

This language, which the Russian Government has proposed as the model for other agreements on liability, has been judged unsatisfactory by the USA, which remains concerned that the language could

---

[149] See note 79.

affect the outcome of any legal action that might be brought in US courts in cases of project-related accidents. For this reason, the USA did not sign the Protocol. Other countries, however, have been prepared to regard signature of the MNEPR Framework Agreement as sufficient basis on which to negotiate and sign the contracts that initiate CTR projects such as submarine dismantlement, and have not waited for it to enter into force.

For projects involving the USA, and for the very large projects anticipated in Russia in the future which carry large risks in case of accident, the guarantees provided in the MNEPR Framework Agreement may need to be supplemented by further and more detailed agreements.

Assistance donors have also objected in cases where equipment or services provided in the framework of CTR projects have been subject to taxes and levies that reduce their overall value and raise the cost of project implementation. In certain cases the duties levied on imported equipment have been 100 per cent of its value—in effect doubling its cost. These levels of duty were established to prevent foreign suppliers from increasing their domestic market share in Russia at the expense of Russian enterprises that manufacture similar equipment. However, Russian laws and regulations make no provision for exemptions for items imported in association with CTR. Again, the Framework Agreement on MNEPR establishes a common position between Russian authorities and assistance donors on this issue.

The immunities contained in the Framework Agreement on MNEPR only apply to nuclear-related projects designated to fall within the Northern Dimension Environmental Programme and are not available for other projects. By modifying Russian legislation the same exemptions and immunities could be provided to all CTR projects. However, while some Russian analysts have argued that it would be preferable to modify the Russian tax code and other regulations, others have pointed out that this could be an uncertain and time-consuming process leading to further delays in project implementation.

Another problem that appears across case studies is the need to make projects compliant with regulations on export control and controls on technology transfer. The national laws of the donor country may require assurances that equipment provided has not been either moved or diverted to an unauthorized use. In the US case the law requires a right of physical access to ensure that end-use assurances have been complied with. In cases where projects are being carried out in locations where access is normally very closely controlled it is necessary to establish at the outset what rules will be acceptable to both sides to avoid subsequent implementation difficulties.

IV. The financial and economic aspects of cooperative threat reduction

The financing of CTR raises a number of separate issues. First, it is necessary to secure a financial commitment large enough to carry out projects while at the same time justifying the cost estimate on which this financial commitment is based. In spite of the emphasis placed on the discussion of the relative value of national efforts to finance CTR, this does not appear to have been a major problem in the past. Second, it is necessary to ensure that financing is available and can be drawn upon when needed. This does seem to have been a difficult problem. There have been numerous examples of allocated funding being returned to national treasuries unspent as a result of a failure to implement elements of a project within the time window before financial authority expired. Third, ensuring that finances are used in the intended manner and for agreed purposes is important because the financial contributors are all accountable to their various domestic authorities. There is anecdotal evidence of a lack of transparency in reporting. However, there does not seem to be evidence that CTR projects have suffered directly from problems of corruption in spite of the poor reputation, in this respect, of the countries in which they have been carried out.

Immediately prior to the 2002 G8 meeting in Kananaskis, and since the establishment of the Global Partnership, a significant element in the discussion of the overall financial aspects of CTR concentrated on whether G8 countries would meet their financial pledges. This discussion has as its background the perception that the USA has carried the principal financial burden for CTR. This perception is, to a certain extent, the product of a particular US view of what constitutes CTR.

The tendency to regard CTR as consisting of those projects of greatest interest to the USA excludes or devalues activities carried out by other countries and in other forums. Moreover, the economic data on CTR is not compiled in a way that permits meaningful comparison. The 'raw' budget numbers for allocations to CTR projects measure inputs rather than outputs from project activities and are not broken down to reflect payments to contractors in donor countries and payments made in the countries where projects are carried out. This approach runs the risk of developing a potentially contentious, and ultimately probably fruitless, discussion about burden sharing within the CTR community. Moreover, it seems to be the case that the financial difficulties are if not a red herring then at least a not insurmountable obstacle to CTR. No technically feasible and politically acceptable projects appear to have stumbled over a lack of financing.

The focus on this issue is also partly a product of Russia's interest in maximizing the transfer of financial resources in connection with projects. The scale of the financing pledged in the context of the G8 Global Partnership has apparently already led to a tendency on the Russian side to discuss the level of economic transfers associated with projects. However, the contracting arrangements used in most CTR projects have meant that the scale of financial flows from donors into Russia has been relatively small. Far more often contributions appear to have been provided by contractors located in the donor country in the form of specific single-use equipment and services that would be inherently difficult to divert or resell.

The fact that projects do not usually involve large-scale cash movements is perhaps also one explanation for the relatively low level of concern about corruption in CTR projects in comparison with other types of external assistance.[150]

In future, the scale of the projects carried out under the overall umbrella of CTR is expected to grow, not least because of the implementation of the G8 Global Partnership. Therefore, the issue of how to manage the financial aspects of CTR is also likely to become a more significant issue. In particular, the question of how to monitor financial transfers connected with project implementation will need to be addressed if there is an increased tendency to opt for contracting

---

[150] However, corruption can have important indirect consequences for CTR. In one example, Japanese legislators blocked project assistance for submarine decommissioning following the discovery that Japanese and Russian officials had colluded to embezzle funds allocated to bilateral development assistance projects that were not in any way related to CTR projects.

arrangements that make greater use of local agencies and companies in the country where the projects are being carried out. In certain respects this would be the most efficient contract model. However, except for very small projects, the authorities in most donor countries have been reluctant to accept arrangements that involve large-scale financial transfers to government agencies or directly to contractors in countries where projects have been carried out. This has been resisted partly because it has been thought to deprive the donor of a useful instrument to ensure project implementation and partly because of the difficulty of satisfying financial audit and accountability requirements in the donor country under this arrangement—including the political need to satisfy national parliaments that resources have been used effectively and honestly.

As the size of individual CTR projects grows, it may be useful to enter into dialogue with the development assistance community, where the skills needed to implement large projects in foreign countries in cooperation with local suppliers have already been developed. In countries where projects will be conducted, notably in Russia, the wider process of developing domestic instruments for auditing and to ensure transparency would increase international confidence in the ability of both government and industry to manage financial transfers in a responsible manner. In future, development of these types of domestic instruments could change external views about the preferred form of financing CTR.

A more pressing problem is the question of how to cost the various elements of a project in a manner that is regarded as fair by all parties. Making an evaluation of the costs of external assistance requires a method for establishing the true costs of project-related tasks. This method might, in future, involve competitive tenders. For example, within the EU one member state might be prepared to open a tender to companies from other member states rather than looking exclusively for domestic suppliers. In order to control project costs a valuation of the external contribution from project participants in the donor countries as well as a fair valuation of the facilities, people, expertise, technology and equipment provided by Russian entities are required. The US General Accounting Office has questioned the reliability of such estimates made in the early stages of projects.[151]

---

[151] US General Accounting Office (GAO), *Weapons of Mass Destruction: Additional Russian Cooperation Needed to Facilitate US efforts to Improve Security at Russian Sites*,

In past projects the value placed by Western partners and Russian partners on contributions from local sources has differed by as much as a factor of 10. In recent years, however, a number of Russian-based entities have developed the skills to value the local content of a range of different international projects. The engagement of these kinds of participants could help to develop a methodology for valuing projects that would make it easier to determine whether partners have met their financial obligations to CTR.

It has been possible for one country to provide the financing for and take responsibility for managing the implementation of short-term, small-scale projects. In such cases the procedures for securing sufficient funds and for managing those funds are already developed within the country concerned. Where projects are larger and more complicated they may stretch the available resources even of larger countries. Many proposed CTR projects are so large that supporting them alone would be beyond the financial means even of the USA.[152]

The implementation of large-scale CTR projects will, in future, require larger contributions from Russia. A significant increase might require new innovations in financing arrangements. One such innovation that is now being evaluated by European governments is the idea of a 'debt swap for non-proliferation'.[153] The Pacific Northwest Center for Global Security[154] first developed the idea of a debt swap, adapting an idea that was first applied to finance environmental projects.[155] Under the debt swap, Western governments would either

GAO-03-482 (GAO: Washington, DC, 24 Mar. 2003), pp. 10–11, URL < http://www.gao. gov>.

[152] Recognition of this difficulty was one part of the USA's motivation in seeking the Global Partnership within the framework of the G8.

[153] The idea is being discussed in the International Working Group (IWG) of the European Nuclear Cities Initiative, an arrangement intended to facilitate European efforts to assist the Russian Federation in converting and downsizing the Russian nuclear weapon complex by assisting with solutions to social and economic problems in Russia's nuclear cities. The IWG is chaired by the European Commission and brings together experts, officials and representatives of governmental entities from Italy, Russia, the UK and the USA as well as representatives from the European Commission, Euratom and the Russian Nuclear Cities.

[154] The Center was established in Oct. 1998 by the US Department of Energy as part of the Pacific Northwest National Laboratory. See URL <http://pnwcgs.pnl.gov/Center/center. htm>.

[155] The practice appears to have been invented in the early 1980s by the World Wildlife Fund, now the Worldwide Fund For Nature. For a generic description of debt swap arrangements see Fuller, J., 'Debt for nonproliferation: the next step in threat reduction', *Arms Control Today*, vol. 32, no. 1 (Jan./Feb. 2002), pp. 22–26. For additional material on debt swaps for non-proliferation see the Pacific Northwest National Laboratory Internet site (note 154).

assume Russian commercial debt to financial institutions or forgive debts where the government is the debt holder. In exchange, the Russian Government would establish an endowment equivalent in value to the debt relieved and use this fund to sponsor CTR projects.

In the USA, where the Senate passed the Debt Reduction and Non-proliferation Act in 2001, there has been considerable interest in widening support for this practice and other countries have been lobbied to examine the proposal. Moreover, in the longer term a strengthened CTR programme may require increased resources that can only be obtained through this kind of arrangement.

The response to this proposal has been lukewarm—not least because financing projects by other means does not appear to have been impossible. West European officials have argued that Russia is able to increase its contributions without such relief, which could send a negative signal about the need to respect financial obligations. Moreover, setting up the debt swap would require officials responsible for CTR in donor countries to engage in considerable contact and persuasion with the holders of the debt in their respective countries.

The cost of the first phase of the programme to manage nuclear environmental problems on the Kola Peninsula has been estimated at $500 million and the full costs, including restoration and nuclear environmental protection, are recognized as likely to be much higher than this amount. In future, the financing of very large projects by European countries is more likely to be achieved by pooling the national CTR resources of participating states in a discretionary fund.

Where projects take more than one year to implement, countries such as Germany have experienced problems with 'rolling over' funds from one year to the next. Money that is not spent in one financial year is lost and has to be re-applied for. For donors facing this type of budget process it would be ideal if projects proceeded according to an agreed and predictable timetable. However, the creation of discretionary funds that can be freed from the financial constraints faced within national budget processes, but that nevertheless still provide assurances that funds will be properly managed, would also be a useful alternative—especially as projects become more complex.

The creation of a discretionary fund, into which resources can be paid but whose payment system is more flexible, is an approach that has been explored in, for example, the PFP Trust Fund and the framework of the NDEP Support Fund.

The PFP Trust Fund has only been used to support projects for landmine clearance and small arms collection and destruction. However, as noted in chapter 2, there is evidence that the NATO programme is expanding its scope to include areas that have more traditionally been considered part of the CTR agenda—such as the safe disposal of missile and rocket fuel. The fund can be applied to projects carried out in any of the countries that are members of the PFP.

As also described in chapter 2, the NDEP has been created to facilitate environmental protection projects in north-western Russia. Its financing might be used in particular for projects related to the management of spent nuclear fuel and other radioactive waste. The NDEP offers several advantages over purely national financing. First, the greater flexibility in using allocated resources would help countries limit the risk that projects would be delayed because allocated but unspent funds had been lost. Second, the NDEP was established through an international agreement that lays out clear rules for fund management. Third, because Russia is a party to the NDEP agreement it has accepted these rules. Fourth, fund management and oversight are carried out by organizations such as the Northern Investment Bank that have experience in the task and enjoy the confidence of countries that contribute to the Support Fund. Moreover, because contributors belong to the NDEP Steering Group, they also receive reports and information on the use of the funds they have contributed.

One disadvantage of the NDEP arrangement is that it is geographically limited. The projects that have been defined as eligible for funding are those carried out in the Northern Dimension area defined by the EU. Furthermore, the NDEP is only intended to help finance nuclear-related projects, and funds would not be available for projects related to CBW.[156]

The EU Action Plan Against Proliferation of Weapons of Mass Destruction[157] anticipates a significant increase in funds for CTR projects after 2006, in line with the decisions made in the framework

---

[156] A specific purpose of the Support Fund is 'to support projects addressing the severe risks of nuclear pollution in the Russian Northern Dimension Area through nuclear safety related projects'. Rules of the Northern Dimension Environmental Partnership Support Fund (note 78), Attachment 1, Article 1, Section 1.02.

[157] See note 49.

of the G8 Global Partnership. Money taken from national contributions from EU member states could also be set aside to create a discretionary fund managed and dispersed by the European Commission, although no decisions of this kind have been taken.[158] Under such an arrangement the day-to-day management of these resources could avoid the problem some countries face with securing national project financing, while the countries would still receive regular information and reports about how their contributions were being used through their participation in the Council of the European Union.

Using the precedent of the 1999 and 2003 Joint Actions,[159] the Commission might also increasingly use its local representation offices to help with aspects of project implementation, including financial management. Under the Joint Action a policy and project coordination section was established at the European Commission in Brussels and a project assistance team was established in Moscow that reports to the Commission. Together, these officials are currently responsible for a range of tasks, including managing contacts with EU member states that contribute funds to a particular project and ensuring close cooperation with personnel working on projects funded by the EU in Russia.[160]

While real, many of the problems associated with the financial management of CTR projects are not specific to CTR but also exist in other large international projects. Development assistance projects, in particular, seem to share many characteristics of CTR projects. Judging from the available information, national and international agencies tasked with overseeing the implementation of development assistance projects, including financial oversight and cash management tasks, appear to have played little if any role in managing CTR projects.

V. Conclusions

There are too few descriptive case studies of projects carried out in countries other than Russia or in Russia by countries other than the

---

[158] This kind of decision would also have to take into account resource implications. However, at present the EU activities related to non-proliferation, arms control, disarmament and export control are undertaken by c. 7 individuals—3 in the Council and 4 in the Commission—and under any likely future scenario this number will have to increase.

[159] See notes 80 and 84.

[160] 'Terms of reference for the unit of experts under the EU Cooperation Programme for Non-proliferation and Disarmament in the Russian Federation', *Official Journal of the European Union*, L 157 (26 June 2003), p. 71.

USA to draw clear conclusions about best practice in project management for general application. However, it is possible to infer some tentative conclusions from the existing material.

National authorities have maintained control over the different aspects of project management and implementation in the past. In future, however, the growing number of projects, and their apparent increased complexity, will make it both more convenient and more necessary to seek joint approaches to project management and administration. These joint approaches would be the best way to ensure the transparency and reciprocity that have sometimes been seen as lacking in CTR.

For the country where projects are being carried out, the development of a national plan to establish the place of CTR as an element of national policy could enhance prospects for the overall success of projects. In their national plan, authorities would need to make clear that they do not see CTR as an opportunity for raising revenue, but rather as an important and necessary part of national policy. The national plan should be developed after widespread consultation but under high-level political guidance. To the extent possible the national legislative framework should be revised to facilitate successful project implementation.

The existence of such a plan, if it helps to generate sufficient confidence among partners that there is genuine shared understanding of the need for CTR, could also help to simplify the legal framework over time. Such a shared understanding would reduce concerns about good-faith project implementation and perhaps thereby reduce the need to agree in detail on binding legal documents to secure access to the information, places, people and resources needed to implement projects.

There are different approaches to the selection of the contractors that will take responsibility for carrying out project tasks. While none of the models is self-evidently the most appropriate choice for all circumstances, in general, projects seem to work best when local expertise is used whenever possible.

4. Conclusions

I. Introduction: defining cooperative threat reduction

While states are responsible for honouring any commitments they make to one another, it has become obvious that they are not always capable of doing so. Where the failure to implement agreed undertakings reflects a lack of financial or technical capacity rather than a deliberate effort to undermine the terms of an agreement, it is preferable for all parties to offer assistance rather than criticism and punishment. In the period after the end of the cold war, a new type of international cooperation appeared. States are now willing to render practical assistance to one another in order to reduce common threats.

This report underlines that, while there are a large number of issues and problems associated with CTR, it can nevertheless be stated confidently that CTR has made and will continue to make an important contribution to managing security.

At the national level, the USA has been at the forefront in defining CTR as a part of its national security strategy. After a period in which its commitment to CTR was called into question, in September 2002 the US National Security Strategy committed the USA to 'enhance diplomacy, arms control, multilateral export controls and threat reduction assistance that impede states and terrorists seeking weapons of mass destruction. . . . We will continue to build coalitions to support these efforts, encouraging their increased political and financial support for nonproliferation and threat reduction programmes'.[161]

The EU has also begun to define CTR as an important element in its emerging security strategy and as part of its strategy against the proliferation of WMD. Moreover, and of critical importance, the Putin Government has reconfirmed that it perceives CTR as an important element in its security policy.

While it has not been possible for this practical assistance to be made available in all cases where it might be required, states have begun to define the scope of application of CTR and to set priorities.

Given the degree of commitment from the states and bodies that will have to play a central role in CTR, the conditions for defining and

---

[161] 'The National Security Strategy of the United States of America', The White House, Washington, DC, Sep. 2002, p. 14, URL <http://www.whitehouse.gov/nsc/nss.pdf>.

implementing projects have probably never been better. In 2003 important decisions were taken that should facilitate the implementation of projects that have been in gestation for a long period. Efforts to decommission nuclear-powered submarines, eliminate surplus HEU stockpiles, find alternative non-military uses for plutonium stocks and destroy CW have all made important progress.

At the same time, the CTR projects that are mature enough for implementation reflect decisions taken in the past and under different conditions. These projects are not necessarily well attuned to the current concerns about proliferation and counter-terrorism.

In the long term, the rationale for CTR, and therefore its long-term prospects for sustainable and successful project implementation, assumes a common appraisal of threats. However, no such common appraisal has been agreed and codified—or even discussed in a systematic manner among the states active in CTR. It is understandable that officials should defer conceptual and definitional discussions if they see the prospect of implementing projects that have been a long time in preparation. However, there are practical reasons for having this discussion sooner rather than later.

As long as the parameters of CTR remain undefined, it may become increasingly difficult for groups such as the G8 to monitor progress in the Global Partnership. For example, a significant proportion of the contribution of the EU is spent on enhancing nuclear reactor safety. This spending is necessary but it is not an essential part of the effort to prevent the proliferation of nuclear weapons, which is a central goal of the Global Partnership. Whether or not this spending is included will make a critical difference to the degree of additional financing which the EU will need to include in its budget for Global Partnership activities. There will have to be a defensible basis for explaining to governments why the various activities they have undertaken do not 'count' against their Global Partnership pledges, given that nuclear safety is specifically referred to in the Kananaskis Summit documents.[162]

A bottom–up approach to definition—inferred from the catalogue of CTR projects undertaken or being planned—would reveal that there is no obvious organizing principle behind what has been done in the past. Threat reduction has been and remains an ad hoc activity that has

[162] See chapter 2, section III and note 107.

been linked to a number of different parts of the overall security agenda, including the enhancement of military security, environmental protection, and nuclear safety and security.

Initiatives intended to eliminate conventional weapons have not usually been considered to be part of the CTR agenda—in spite of the fact that the characteristics of a number of programmes to locate, secure and destroy conventional arms are very similar to CTR programmes. However, the growing emphasis on counter-terrorism has begun to erode this barrier by gradually bringing, for example, MANPADS that might be used against civil aviation into the remit of measures discussed in forums such as the G8.

To the extent that armed conflict and state collapse in the developing world are recognized as contributing to the causes of and opportunities for terrorism, the relationship of the stockpiles and flows of small arms and light weapons to such conflicts also draws projects to secure and destroy SALW into the sphere of relevance.

While addressing environmental and nuclear safety problems had a value per se in the European context, cooperation to address or solve mutual challenges was partly pursued in the belief that human contacts and improved relations below the state level would help to build a more prosperous and politically stable Russia. During the 1990s, CTR activities were progressively made part of a broader effort to develop cooperation in a number of areas, including several of growing relevance in a security environment where countering terrorist acts committed using WMD or radiological weapons is a prominent feature. These areas include enhancing cooperation on public health issues, with a specific focus on communicable disease; combating organized crime, including illicit trafficking; and developing an integrated border management system to facilitate cross-border human contact and commerce while reducing risks from organized crime and terrorism. In this respect, in particular locations, especially in Russia, CTR broadens to encompass the improvement of political relations, stimulating economic and industrial development, and alleviating social and humanitarian problems.

While at any particular time, because of the need to respond to particular events, one of these areas may receive more attention than others, over time they are not hierarchical. Therefore, the definition of CTR should not be linked too closely to any one problem, however pressing. At the same time, CTR should not become a term that is used so flexibly as to reflect all of the multiple opinions about what constitutes a threat.

To find the correct balance the definition of CTR thus has to be functional rather than grounded in geography or technology. The evaluation carried out in this report tends to confirm the need to define CTR as including any practical measures jointly implemented on the territory of one state by a coalition of parties that may include states, international organizations, local and regional government, NGOs and the private sector, provided that these practical measures are undertaken with the objective of enhancing security.

The absence of a coherent agreed framework makes it impossible to choose one critical area in which all international efforts will be concentrated. Given that there are different perspectives between countries that are critical actors about which problems are of central importance, this lack of a durable agreement that one problem is of central importance is not fatal to CTR. Instead, it suggests that a degree of specialization should be developed within a broad framework.

This approach to definition would facilitate the sectorization of CTR so that different countries and bodies can take a lead in different geographical and technical areas while still being able to make an effective contribution across the overall spectrum of problems. In order that contributions can be maximized a number of issues and problems need to be addressed. The discussion of future developments can be organized under three broad headings: establishing a coherent agenda, implementing agreed projects successfully and evaluating the overall programme to apply lessons learned—thereby further increasing effectiveness.

II. The importance of an overarching framework of agreements

While there is no common appraisal of threats among states, various agreements codify commitments that the overwhelming majority of states agree are beneficial from their national standpoint. The existence of these agreements gives some coherence to CTR.

The existence of an overarching agreement is not a prerequisite for all CTR. Some short-term projects have been conducted on an ad hoc basis. These have usually been designed to address a very specific problem that emerges at a time when governments are sensitized to the potential negative impact of failing to act quickly. An example would be various projects carried out at short notice to remove orphan radiological sources from locations where there is doubt about the capacity of government authorities to organize safe and secure storage locally.

These emergency-type measures notwithstanding, the success of longer and more comprehensive CTR projects intended to address the problems of a particular country appears to correlate with the adequacy of the overarching framework created by international agreements. Where agreements have created clear and agreed objectives and established rules to govern questions such as information exchange and site access, it has been much easier to define CTR projects. On the other hand, where objectives are unclear or contested, progress with project definition and implementation has been either slow, unsatisfactory or often impossible.

One conclusion that can be drawn is that, in future, CTR should not be pursued as an alternative to seeking progress in various international and multilateral frameworks. On the contrary, progress in multilateral processes will play a useful facilitating role in CTR. There are a number of areas in which these types of linkages should be explored more actively than at present.

Some elements of CTR assume that certain weapons are surplus to requirements. However, in the absence of agreements it is not possible to determine what is surplus and therefore available for destruction, neutralization or conversion. While CTR clearly requires the consent of the authorities of the country in which projects will be carried out, and cannot be imposed, it is equally clear that in practice donor governments see it as an opportunity to influence the choices of those authorities through dialogue. Donors do not simply accept the catalogue of projects put to them without discussion.

In the area of arms control, the CWC has made a major contribution to the success of CTR projects. Other countries where CW programmes will need to be dismantled do not appear to need the same kinds of assistance that Russia has been receiving in order to comply with the convention. However, to facilitate new CTR projects additional progress is required in the BW and the nuclear weapon areas.

Without this element of diplomatic 'give and take', it will be difficult to maintain the linkage between CTR and tackling the threat of proliferation to states and terrorist groups. This is because some of the most serious proliferation concerns exist around issues and in locations where CTR projects have been most difficult to develop.

While CTR projects may have provided an indirect means to discover more about Russian BW capacities, they have been no more successful in resolving remaining concerns in this area than other processes. In the area of BW a decision on how to resolve the problem of Russia's status regarding the BTWC would open the way for practical cooperation that could reduce proliferation risks.

Senator Sam Nunn, one of the leading figures behind CTR, has stated that 'the most effective, least expensive way to prevent nuclear terrorism is to secure nuclear weapons and materials at the source'.[163] However, under current conditions, CTR programmes cannot secure Russian nuclear weapons, while there are many more sources of weapon-grade and weapon-usable nuclear material than Russian stockpiles.

Further agreements on reductions to nuclear weapon arsenals, other than those currently subject to the Russian–US SORT Treaty, as well as agreement to ban the production of fissile materials for use in nuclear weapons could lead to progress that would enhance the prospects for successful CTR projects and also address concerns about proliferation to states or to groups planning to carry out mass-impact terrorist acts.

Recent experience suggests that important states—most notably Russia and the USA—have not seen sufficient reason to modify their national security policies and plans in ways that could facilitate such agreements. In time, the clear and demonstrable link between successful arms control and the successful implementation of practical measures of great mutual interest to Russia and the USA might help to bring about a renewed commitment to future progress.

Apart from arms control, the agreements that are currently being discussed to create a more comprehensive set of rules on nuclear safety and security are being modified to take into account the current

---

[163] Nunn S., Remarks at the Conference on Strengthening the Global Partnership Project, London, 20 Jan. 2003, URL <http://www.sgpproject.org/events/sam_nunn_remarks.html>. A former US Senator, Sam Nunn is co-chairman of the Nuclear Threat Initiative (see notes 5 and 55).

threat environment. There is considerable political momentum behind the process now being conducted within the IAEA to modify a number of important conventions that establish agreed standards in this area. Once this process is concluded, it should be of great help with establishing CTR priorities and defining the practical details of projects that can help to implement the conventions.

In the area of BW-related agreements there appears to be much less momentum and a risk that what Amy Smithson has called an 'uneven patchwork' is being developed that could be exploited fairly easily by proliferators and terrorists.[164] There is an emerging view that it will be necessary to strengthen bio-safety and bio-security. The entry into force of the September 2003 Cartagena Protocol on Biosafety to the 1992 Convention on Biological Diversity can be seen as one step in the process of creating a more common framework for regulations.[165] The protocol is intended to help ensure an adequate level of protection in the field of the safe transfer, handling and use of living modified organisms resulting from modern biotechnology, taking into account risks to human health, and specifically focusing on cross-border transfers. However, in comparison with the nuclear safety and nuclear security fields, the framework of agreed rules and the capacities of specialized agencies are much weaker. Moreover, while rules and procedures to oversee and regulate biological research have been developed nationally, there is no international agreement on what such rules and procedures should cover.[166]

In Europe, the EU is likely to develop common rules and regulations to govern these issue areas. The enlargement of the EU might mean that CTR assistance to member states could be arranged when it is needed either at the EU level using common resources or between EU member states. More broadly, the European integration process might lead to a regional approach to CTR as additional states outside the EU receive assistance to harmonize their national rules, policies and procedures to emerging EU standards. Countries in south-eastern

---

[164] Smithson, A. E., Prepared Statement Before the Senate Committee on Foreign Relations, Washington, DC, 19 Mar. 2003, URL <http://foreign.senate.gov/testimony/2003/SmithsonTestimony.030319.pdf>. Amy E. Smithson is the former Director of the Chemical and Biological Weapons Nonproliferation Project at the Henry L. Stimson Center.

[165] The text of the protocol on Biosafety and of other related materials are available at URL <http:/www.biodiv.org/biosafety/protocol.asp>.

[166] Kellman, B. and Müthe-Lindgren, O., 'Summary of national laws and measures for counter terrorism regulation of biology', Unpublished manuscript, Programme on Preventing Disease Weaponization, Aug. 2003.

Europe as well as Belarus, Moldova and Ukraine might be addressed using such an approach. The EU is in the process of strengthening the security element of its dialogue with Russia, and this will include a more significant role for CTR.

III. Coordination of cooperative threat reduction

While the existence of international agreements can give coherence to CTR, the problem remains that not all of the commitments contained in different agreements are fully compatible with one another. The agreements in the areas of arms control, environmental protection, and nuclear safety and security were developed by different officials at various times and reflect different conditions. While the fact that they are not fully consistent is not surprising, it does mean that there is a requirement for a coordinating mechanism to provide coherence in finding, facilitating and financing the projects carried out under the broad CTR umbrella. At a minimum, projects carried out for one pur-pose should not undermine the effort to implement another part of the same overall security agenda.

At the national level, states are beginning to review their overall approach to CTR and to coordinate the actions of different parts of government in this area. Ideally, the coordination process should inte-grate planning, budgeting, implementation and project evaluation into a single system. However, while this might be attempted nationally during the next few years, recreating this level of integration is not realistic at the international level.

In the immediate future there will inevitably be some overlaps and duplication in the process—although the process of thinking through national positions gives reason to believe that improved international coherence can be achieved over time.

Currently, states are not proactive in identifying CTR projects. The existing donor mechanisms should allow states to evaluate requests for assistance that are put to them against the background of more complete information. However, no overall inventory of problems that need to be solved has been created. This kind of inventory could facilitate *cooperative threat prevention*. It could be the basis for more active approaches to states in order to investigate the prospects for developing projects when problems are believed to exist that, if not addressed, could have a wider impact. It could also be an instrument for tackling arms-related concerns for peace-building after conflicts.

Most of the energies of current mechanisms have been put into facilitating the definition and implementation of project ideas that have been put to them by states, most notably by Russia. There are a number of bodies currently undertaking the task of trying to coordinate the various CTR projects under discussion. It has been demonstrated that the existing mechanisms are flexible enough in their geographical coverage, mandate and working procedures to be able to coordinate planned activities.

From this it can be concluded that no additional coordination mechanisms are needed. However, as the anticipated expansion in CTR takes place, governments will need to keep in mind the fact that these existing mechanisms are available and to use them to a greater extent.

The G8 Senior Officials Group has already demonstrated that it has a valuable role to communicate problems with projects that cannot be resolved at operational level for consideration by senior decision makers. For example, by facilitating the Framework Agreement on MNEPR the G8 allowed an important step to be taken towards a more comprehensive legal basis for projects. That said, there remains much to do before the agreed rules that can already be applied in projects carried out in certain technical areas and with certain countries are available to all projects and all donor countries.

Although the nature of the G8 puts practical limits on the resources that can be devoted to public diplomacy, there is a need for greater clarity or, if the current arrangements are already clear to the participants, greater transparency. The participating states have made clear that they do not see the G8 as an executive body. However, given the wide range of projects that could fall within the scope of the Global Partnership, there is a need to establish a list of priorities and a timetable for implementing agreed projects. Because the Senior Officials Group brings together representatives at sufficiently senior level to take decisions on behalf of their respective governments, the G8 is the appropriate place to attempt this exercise.

While the Senior Officials Group has already become a forum for exchanging information and bringing problems to the attention of senior decision makers to reduce implementation obstacles, there are now three parallel processes taking place under the auspices of the G8. In addition to the Global Partnership, the G8 has initiated processes related to nuclear safety and the physical protection of radiological sources. The manner in which these processes relate to each other in practical terms and the division of labour between them is not clear. The intergovernmental coordination arrangements within NATO and the UN are currently underutilized. Stockpiles of relevant equipment, technology and expertise were not confined to Russia. The Global Partnership already anticipates an expansion of the geographical scope of the projects to be considered within its overall work programme. However, it will be difficult for an informal arrangement with little administrative capacity such as the G8 to cope with conditions in which it has to manage discussions with a large number of countries simultaneously.

A stronger role for the IAEA within CTR seems likely to go hand in hand with the development of agreements in the area of nuclear safety and security, including the physical protection of nuclear and radiological materials. Therefore, it will be important for states to honour their pledges to provide the necessary assistance to the IAEA. This assistance is not only financial but also includes identifying national experts and assets that can be included in the international project teams, which the IAEA is increasingly likely to have to create and coordinate, and ensuring that these assets are available when needed.

The scope for projects in the area of practical disarmament and under the auspices of the PFP seems to be particularly wide given the progressively expanded technical coverage of CTR. In NATO there is a precedent for expanding the terms of reference of the PFP Trust Fund to incorporate new kinds of practical assistance projects.

Within the EU there is a marked tendency to use existing processes to facilitate cooperation both among member states and with the European Commission. For example, the Commission is the only actor that participates in the G8, the Northern Dimension (including NDEP and MNEPR), the European Nuclear Cities Initiative, the ISTC and the Science and Technology Center in Ukraine. At the same time, there are other processes where the Commission is not present (such as the UN) but which the EU has become accustomed to participating in through actions organized by the country chairing the Council of the European Union. Given that this more extensive participation by the EU now clearly appears to be part of a broader development of greater coherence and weight in the overall area of security policy, there is a great deal of logic in developing a critical mass of experts by linking the resources of the Council and the Commission more effectively.[167]

Perhaps surprisingly, this report draws the conclusion that, in the past, the financing of projects was not a major obstacle to their implementation. On the contrary, there are more cases of CTR project money going unspent than cases of good projects falling through for lack of a sponsor.

This finding needs to be qualified, however. It is a misconception that CTR leads to large-scale financial transfers. Most past contributions have been in kind through the provision of equipment and technical assistance. Moreover, in spite of the large sums of up to $20 billion being discussed in the framework of the G8, there is no reason to believe that anything like this amount of money will actually be transferred to Russia over the next 10 years. It is probable that the focus on the pledges made in the G8 context has temporarily diverted Russian attention from this reality. In general, the sums allocated under the Global Partnership should be seen as a proxy for the level of political commitment to projects by donors.

Projects supported in the past, such as technical analyses and feasibility studies, have provided knowledge that is likely to be applied in a number of future projects. The pledges made in the framework of the G8 would seem to provide sufficient financing to cover the costs of projects currently anticipated. However, while in the past the availability of financing for projects was not the main obstacle to their implementation, additional resources could certainly be required should there be a very significant increase in the number of proposals for projects. The more serious financial problems appear to arise at the project level rather than at the wider level of securing macro-commitments from states.

IV. Project implementation

The consent and cooperation of the national authorities in the country where a project is implemented are imperative, and this report sug-

---

[167] The establishment of a joint European External Action Service under the European External Representative is envisaged in The European Convention, Final Report of Working Group 7 on External Action, CONV 459/02, Brussels, 16 Dec 2002.

gests that the approach adopted by these authorities is the single most critical factor in project implementation. A question in the minds of many was the one posed by Kenneth Luongo, 'What will Russia do both politically and financially to make this process work efficiently and to clear away the impediments to progress that have developed over the past 10 years?'[168]

The failure to develop a coherent national approach to CTR greatly increased the difficulties of project implementation in Russia. Agencies and individuals at the national, regional and city administrative levels took decisions that hampered the development and implementation of projects (or alternatively refused to take decisions) because they evaluated what was required of them against the narrow interests of their particular institution, without a wider understanding of the process they were being asked to contribute to.

Russia has taken steps to facilitate CTR as part of the wider process of improving relations with the USA in particular and the West in general. The best way to increase the overall effectiveness of the process would be for this more coherent national approach to be codified. At the same time there still appears to be disagreement about the extent to which the Russian administrative arrangements currently in place are optimal.

A case can be made for the creation of a single body that is competent to take decisions and perform tasks that facilitate project implementation and that is known to be responsible for these tasks. This could mean a CTR 'Tsar', the establishment of a body under the direct control of the executive leadership of the country, or a specialized inter-agency body. This, in turn, could simplify the performance of tasks that have been difficult in the past, such as collecting information and collating it into reports for distribution to donors, and addressing practical questions that otherwise require contractors to make multiple applications to different bodies (e.g., who should be granted site access). However, the experience of some countries has been that centralization can lead to a remoteness from the real problems facing projects and that this kind of arrangement, while conceptually appealing, might not work in practice. In a country like Russia these feelings are compounded by past administrative practice and by geography.

---

[168] Luongo (note 90).

In contrast, the development of relations with direct beneficiaries of CTR assistance has, perhaps not surprisingly, been much more positive. This leads to the conclusion that projects should be implemented as close to the ground as possible, preferably by mixed, international teams. Critics of this approach argue that it is unrealistic in a country such as Russia to believe that such a devolved approach would be acceptable to agencies that and individuals who are accustomed to close control of both decision-making authority and information.

Projects can be considered a success in their own terms yet still give little information about the overall extent of national capacities in the country in which they are being carried out—this is, in fact, one of the reasons why it has been possible to overcome the preconception in the Russian military establishment that CTR is a cover for espionage. Therefore, binding commitments on site access or access to documents should not be a condition for carrying out CTR.

The best solution to all such problems would be a mutually supportive and comprehensive set of international agreements on arms control, CTR, environmental protection, and nuclear safety and security. Pending such agreements, the procedures for information gathering and reporting will play a critical role in creating confidence in implementation, and support for future projects, in conditions where on-site verification of performance might not be possible.

A procedure through which direct meetings can be arranged between representatives of donor states and the individuals responsible for project implementation (which does not only mean the managers of agencies, facilities and enterprises but quite probably also their staff) might be a way of satisfying all parties that their interests are being respected. This kind of access would both facilitate information exchange and build confidence in project implementation.

In conclusion, the political prospects for developing effective CTR are currently favourable. States are putting in place the necessary administrative and financial resources to translate political commitments into project activities. Under these circumstances, CTR seems certain to play a valuable role alongside other measures in managing threats of current concern.

Index

Luongo, Kenneth 47, 112

Maastrict Treaty (1993) 43
MANPADS (man-portable air defence
weapons) 59–60, 61, 67–68, 103
missile delivery systems 2, 6
MNEPR (Multilateral Nuclear
Environmental Programme in Russia):
Committee 42
Framework Agreement 38, 41–42, 51,
92, 99, 109:
Protocol to 41, 91–92
Global Partnership and 51
Moldova 72, 107
Murmansk Trilateral Initiative (1994)
36–37

NATO (North Atlantic Treaty
Organization):
arms control and 69
CTR and 69–73, 74–75, 110
Defence Planning and Operations
Division 71
demilitarization and 70–71, 72
EU and 73
Information, Consultation and
Training Centre 70
Maintenance and Supply Agency
(NAMSA) 71–72, 74
Partnership for Peace 70, 71, 110:
Trust Fund 72, 98, 110
PMSC 70, 72
project management 69, 71, 72
proliferation and 69, 70
Senior Political Committee 70
Senior Politico-Military Group on
Proliferation (SGP) 69, 70
Weapons of Mass Destruction Centre
69–70
NATO–Russia Council 70
NDEP (Northern Dimension
Environmental Partnership) 40–41, 42,
98
Netherlands 1, 27, 40, 42, 78
Niger 68
Nonproliferation and Disarmament
Cooperation Initiative (NDCI, 2001)
27, 28

Nordic Investment Bank 40
northern Europe:
cooperation 18, 19, 36–39
CTR and 18
environmental protection 19
groupings 19
Northern Investment Bank 98
Norway 1, 18, 36, 37, 40, 53, 57, 64, 74
NPT (Non-Proliferation Treaty, 1968)
13
nuclear material:
accountancy 40, 66
explosive constructed from 21–22
Global Partnership and 49
from nuclear weapons 5
'orphan' radiological sources 66, 105
proliferation risk 7
security of 15, 16, 21–24, 30, 66
nuclear plants:
attack on 22
decommissioning 18
Russian designed 17, 18
security and 23, 66
nuclear safety 6, 17–19, 89, 102, 103,
106
nuclear submarines:
decommissioning 20, 29, 42, 54, 61,
87, 94 fn. 102, 149
dismantling 53–54, 75
waste fuel from 20, 37, 42
reactors 7
Nuclear Threat Initiative 29–30
nuclear waste:
cleaning up 41, 61
dumping of 19–20
management of 38, 39, 40, 41
security of 7, 22, 23, 24
treatment of 36–37, 38, 41
nuclear weapons:
CTR and 1, 2, 4, 6, 9, 106
dismantled 47
security 9
Global Partnership and 49
missile delivery systems 6, 7, 12, 13,
87
security of 5, 6
nuclear weapons, dismantled: nuclear
material from 7, 47